GO BIG OR GO HOME

GO
BIG
OR GO
HOME

5 **WAYS TO CREATE A CUSTOMER EXPERIENCE**
THAT WILL CLOSE THE DEAL

DIANA KANDER
TUCKER TROTTER

HOUNDSTOOTH
PRESS

Hardcover ISBN: 978-1-5445-3637-8
Paperback ISBN: 978-1-5445-3636-1
Ebook ISBN: 978-1-5445-3635-4
Audiobook ISBN: 978-1-5445-3638-5

CONTENTS

TEXT THE AUTHORS WHILE YOU READ

We got this idea when Diana's friend Sabrina was reviewing an early draft of the book and just couldn't help but live-text her thoughts. Sabrina shared her favorite stories and takeaways and of course examples from her own career of the principles mentioned throughout the book.

The conversation that ensued was so fun and gave us so many insights and ideas for the next version of the book that we wanted to replicate it with each and every reader!

So as you are enjoying the following pages and you feel compelled to text the authors, simply text 816-399-0084 and we will reply as much as we are able ☺.

Is this a crazy idea or the best idea? Only one way to find out!

IF IT'S NOT MEMORABLE, IT'S MEDIOCRE

Here's the Big Idea in Seventy-Nine Words

How do underdogs close huge deals they have no business winning? How do rainmakers pull off a sale before the RFP is ever issued? They don't do it with a logical argument or even the best PowerPoint presentation. They do it by designing an irresistible pitch that makes the customer think, "This just *feels* right." This book is your blueprint for creating the memorable presentation that will speak to your customer on a subconscious level and seal the deal!

If it's not memorable, it's mediocre.

We all need to take a deep breath, hold hands, and admit that the current model of business presentations is broken.

In 2010, Diana was consulting with a large healthcare client in search of a new law firm. The client planned to spend millions of dollars in legal fees per year. On this particular day, Diana was facilitating the interviews of the three finalists, representing some of the nation's top law firms.

The first group of lawyers strode into the conference room. There were five of them, all in expensive suits. They unlatched their briefcases, and the lead lawyer stood and launched into his pitch. He was indisputably compelling. He explained that there were three reasons to pick his firm:

First, their expertise in healthcare law. Second, they were the oldest law firm west of the Mississippi, with well over a century of experience and prestige. Third, they prided themselves on being "business-minded." The clients nodded along, very impressed.

When it was over, Diana escorted the lawyers out. They were smiling, they swaggered, they were high-fiving—they knew they'd crushed it.

A few minutes later, Diana brought in the next firm. Their pitch was confident, practiced, persuasive. They presented three reasons to hire their firm. They described the depth of their expertise in healthcare law, how their law firm was over a hundred years old, and how often their clients praised them for being so "business-minded."

Diana looked around the room. Had anyone else noticed that this second law firm had given the same three reasons to pick them as the first firm? It was hard to tell.

As Diana escorted them out, she noted the laughter and fist bumps. They were feeling the glow that comes from acing a presentation, like warm sunlight on your face. In came the third firm, every bit as polished and professional as the first two.

"First," the lead lawyer began, "this firm has been a pillar of this community for six generations. Second, we are nationally renowned for our healthcare expertise. And third, unlike other firms, we are business-focused—we don't just help you find the legal solution; we help you find the business one."

Diana led the smiling team out of the room. When she came back, the clients were quiet. There were eight decision makers around the table, tasked with finding the right firm to steer their organization into the future. Diana tried to break the silence.

"So," she asked, "how did they do?"

Diana saw a lot of nods and smiles. "They were all very good," someone said.

"Okay," she said. "Anything we didn't like?"

"No, they were fine," said one. "Well…that one group was all wearing bow ties. That was odd."

"But that other group," said someone else, "they kept saying 'my partner so-and-so.' It was all weirdly formal. I just don't know that that's a great fit for us."

One after another, they chimed in, each trying to come up with anything that could help them decide between three eerily similar pitches. Finally, someone shrugged and asked, "So what *are* their rates?"

And just like that, each of these century-old law firms turned into mere commodities, like brands of toothpaste on a supermarket shelf. The problem wasn't that anyone had blown their presentation. It was that **each one had failed to stand out.** They were perfectly mediocre.

Unfortunately, the law firms' approach isn't unusual—it's the norm. We've all been guilty of putting together a presentation that's beautifully polished, one that checks every box and answers every question—and stopping there. But the fact is, our competitors are doing exactly the same thing.

How do you prevent such inadvertently mediocre presentations? Diana witnessed it happen but had no idea what the firms could have done better until ten years later, when she met Tucker. Tucker is the CEO of Dimensional Innovations (DI), an experience design firm that's been on the Inc. 5000 list of the fastest growing companies in America for the last seven years. He was considering writing a book about how DI creates remarkable experiences and a mutual friend thought Diana might walk him through the process, having written two books previously herself. As Diana was taking a tour of the company's 200,000 square-foot fabrication facility, Tucker pointed to a mammoth structure that looked like a space-age ranch-style house. "That's the world's largest 3D printer. We bought it to make the Raiders' torch for their new stadium."

Everything about what he was saying felt colossal. From the immense machine to the nine-story torch DI had built. Diana had so many questions but decided to start with something simple: "How did you get that project?" she asked.

"Oh, it's a great story. We actually have an internal process on the pitches that really matter. We designate them an LTF and we go all out to close the deal. We go the extra mile to create magic and trust. It's not easy, but our CFO says that while our usual close rate on pitches is about 45 percent, when we designate something an LTF, it goes to 90 percent."

Diana was finally able to look away from the 3D printer. "Ninety percent of the hardest-to-win pitches?"

Tucker chuckled. "Yeah, I guess you could put it that way."

"And LTF. What does that stand for?"

Tucker smiled. "Land The Fucker."

DI had a secret sauce. Not just for creating experiences for their clients but also for closing the biggest deals. And Diana became obsessed with understanding exactly how and why it worked. How do you purposefully create magic? Or trust? Diana interviewed team members from every department. She talked to DI clients. And what she found was a very deliberate, systematic approach to creating pitches that were experiences themselves, ones that created **strong emotional connections.**

Emotional Connection Drives Your Customers to Act

The law firms all tailored their pitches to decision makers who they thought would act in a logical way, weighing cost and benefit and choosing the optimal option. That's the image of the ideal executive: cool, savvy, and unflappably rational.

Unfortunately, that's not how humans make decisions. Right out of the gate, let's put this false belief to bed: no matter how logical you think a customer is, **emotion guides every buying decision they make**—and the bigger the decision, the more powerful the emotional component.

According to Harvard Business School professor Gerald Zaltzman, 95 percent of our purchase decision making takes place in the subconscious mind[1]—specifically, they're driven by our emotions. Most of our "rational decisions" are just gut instincts that our brain rationalizes after the fact.

Researchers at Baylor College of Medicine submitted sixty-seven subjects to the time-honored taste test: Coke or Pepsi?[2] First, the test was blind, meaning that the labels were hidden from participants, and Pepsi won by a mile. But when the researchers showed the subjects the company logos *before* they drank, the results flipped: Coke crushed Pepsi.

During the test, they scanned the subjects' brains and discovered that seeing the familiar red-and-white Coke label sparked a lot of activity in certain emotionally sensitive parts of the brain that governed memory and behavior control. The Pepsi label, however, did nothing. So even when they consciously preferred the taste of Pepsi, the participants' emotional memories of Coke's logo were so powerful that their subconscious brain convinced them otherwise.

Countless other research studies have demonstrated all kinds of completely irrational decision making:

- We declare that food tastes better when it is more expensive.[3]

- Individuals buy name-brand medications at the drugstore even though identical and cheaper generics are available.[4]

- Placebos work on patients *even when they know* they are ingesting sugar pills.[5]

Marketers have long been aware of the need to engage the customers' emotions. That's why they are so determined to present every product as an experience. It's not a bottle of Herbal Essences shampoo anymore; it's a naked sensuous romp through a rainforest. It's not a tube of Preparation H; it's the sweet cool relief of sitting on a cloud. It's often ridiculous, but at least marketers understand the power of creating an experience. In-person business pitches lag far behind in this respect.

The reason most pitches look a lot like the very competent and mediocre law firms' is because **we're fooling ourselves about how we make our own purchasing decisions.**

If we tell ourselves that we buy rationally, we'll expect others to do the same, and what we miss is that our subconscious decision making is running circles around our conscious brain. Researchers watching individuals' brains in an fMRI machine found that they could predict the outcome of a simple decision up to eleven seconds before the subject themselves realized it.[6] That's because our subconscious first decides and later communicates it to the rational brain, at which point the rational brain comes up with all kinds of reasons for why the decision was a good one.

Business *Is* Personal

At this point, you may be thinking, "Sure, consumers are emotionally malleable. But surely, *businesses* are better at making purely rational decisions?"

First of all, until the artificial intelligence apocalypse arrives, businesses are run by humans. So all of the same neuroscience principles apply to them, no matter how prestigious their titles.

Second, it turns out that emotional connection is even *more* important in the B2B setting. A joint study between Google and CEB discovered that B2B customers actually value their emotional connections to vendors and service providers significantly more than consumers do.[7]

The reason for this is that B2B purchases involve *far* more risk than ordinary consumer purchases. If you go to a store and buy something that turns out to be lousy, you can usually just take it back. But if you buy a shipment of microchips or hire a contractor for a multimillion-dollar construction project, there's no margin for error. That's why B2B purchasers are almost 50 percent more likely to buy a product or service when they have an emotional connection to the vendor.

The higher the stakes, the *more* we rely on our emotions and intuition to guide us and the more we need that gut feeling that tells us something is the right choice.

The good news is that we can plan for those gut feelings. That's what DI has figured out.

> Everyone has a compelling case.
> But compelling cases don't close the big deals;
> emotional experiences do.

Diana's past books had nothing to do with sales pitches. Her previous titles taught businesses how to ask better questions to innovate products and services and create a culture of curiosity. But as she was learning more and more about the DI method, she started applying the principles to her own business. She immediately felt those emotional connections and closed a lot more deals. Diana was hooked. She told Tucker that she *had* to co-author this book just to have the opportunity to learn more about why DI's methodology was so effective and to seek out examples of how others have used the same principles.

The Go Big or Go Home Blueprint

Whatever industry you're in, whether you're running a bare-bones startup or hunting new opportunities for an established company, your goal in crafting a presentation is a simple one. It's to connect with the client on a subconscious level and remove any possibility that they might choose someone else.

And here's the thing: if you're *not* doing these things, you're gambling that no one else is either. Because if you show up with an ordinary compelling pitch and someone else took the time to create an emotional experience, you're definitely going home emptyhanded.

To Go Big or Go Home means to put your all into a presentation. If you really care about this deal, if you really want to demonstrate to this audience that they matter to you, then you can't just copy and paste your last presentation and insert a new logo on the first page.

It's not enough just to want to be remarkable. You need to purposefully weave moments of magic into your presentation. Magic to help you connect, build trust, and keep their attention on what you have to say.

The next chapter will explain why these moments of magic are vital to a successful pitch, and the chapters that follow will each offer a tool you can use to create that emotional connection and make the customer want to find a way to say yes!

To help you remember them, each tool starts with one of the letters in the word MAGIC.

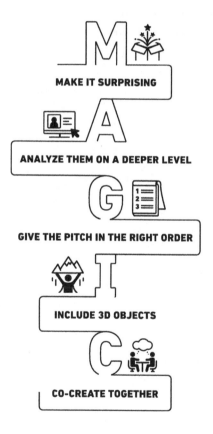

MAKE IT SURPRISING

ANALYZE THEM ON A DEEPER LEVEL

GIVE THE PITCH IN THE RIGHT ORDER

INCLUDE 3D OBJECTS

CO-CREATE TOGETHER

DOWNLOAD THIS POSTER AND OTHER HELPFUL TOOLS AT GOBIGBONUS.COM

We're excited to go on this ride with you. Please know this: you're holding in your hands an unprecedented collection of some of the most memorable pitches in film, sports, business, and philanthropy. These stories come from individuals and organizations that decided to Go Big or Go Home because their deals were important. They mattered. One day, you'll have a pitch that matters too. And when you do, you can follow the simple steps outlined in this book to channel all of your enthusiasm into an experience that will seal the deal!

CHAPTER 2

WHY MOMENTS OF MAGIC ARE ESSENTIAL

People don't pay attention to boring things.

The average SAT essay takes about thirty minutes to write. Want to guess how long it takes to grade?

Five minutes? Ten?

According to a veteran SAT essay reviewer, about forty-five seconds.[8]

The trick is that SAT readers aren't looking at what was written, only *how*. Their job is to essentially scan the page looking to see that students satisfy the test's requirements: Is there a thesis statement stating a clear position? Two specific examples? A brief conclusion? Is the language sophisticated or crude? Is the sentence structure complex or basic? These questions determine the student's grade, so it is all the readers care about. Moreover, most of the reviewers find that the instant they finish grading an essay, they immediately forget what was in it. The only ones they seem to remember are the trainwrecks or the ones that made them laugh, and the trainwrecks are a lot more common.

We spend most of our workdays on autopilot, doing whatever the equivalent of grading an SAT essay is—tasks that we are so used to doing that we don't really have to think very hard about them. It's an emotionally neutral state. That's why we don't remember most of what we do on a given day. This is especially true for people who are on the receiving end of a *lot* of sales presentations.

If you only pitch the way your audience expects you to pitch, they're not really going to be listening to what you're saying, only *how* you're saying it. And later, when they talk about your pitch, they're going to be talking about how they started counting the number of times you said "Let me be clear" or how they couldn't stop watching the vein on the side of your neck bulge. What they won't remember, though, is anything you said.

Psychologists have long understood that **we forget about 50 percent of new information within an hour** of hearing it.[9] That goes up to 70 percent within twenty-four hours and **90 percent after a week.**[10] This is a death sentence for most B2B (or as some call them, "Boring to Boring") presentations, because by the time your potential client has met with all the potential vendors and is ready to make a decision, they've already forgotten most of the compelling arguments you made.

THE FORGETTING CURVE

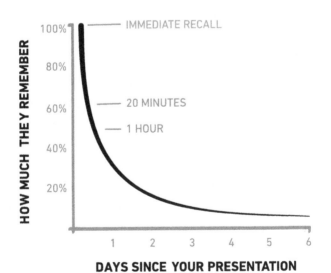

Fortunately, the rate at which our prospects forget can be significantly influenced by the amount of emotion we can trigger in our pitch. This explains why you have such vivid memories of every part of September 11, 2001, and why you can remember the weather on your wedding day, but you have no idea what happened on August 11, 2001, and you likely don't remember the weather just one month ago. **The higher the emotional peak, the deeper a memory will sear into our brains.**[11]

Go Big or Go Home pitches are designed to create these emotional peaks. We call them magic moments. They are like a refresh button for the attention span.

Magic moments force the customer to disengage their autopilot system and give you their full attention.

Now think back to the lawyers' presentations to the healthcare company. There were no unpleasant moments. The pitches were fine. The clients even enjoyed meeting them. But **enjoyment is *standard*, and standard isn't memorable.** None of the teams created even a single magic moment that changed how the clients *felt*, and as a result, their enduring memory of the presentation was the experience of feeling *nothing*, which is the worst possible outcome from a presentation. **If you're not creating emotional peaks, you'll never be memorable—you'll just be another commodity, reduced to competing on price.**

That's why, when creating an experience, you must ask two questions: First, what can you do to deliver that emotional punch? And two, *when* will you do it? A lot of professionals talk about how they want the audience to feel at the end of a presentation. But none of us "feel" anything for more than a few seconds. And **if you can't quite tell when your emotional peaks take place, then *you don't have any*.**

We suggest that when preparing your pitch, you should literally map out the emotional moments of the presentation. We've included the template that we use on the next page.

Graphing it out visually doesn't just help you tell where the peaks of your presentation are; it also lets you know the valleys—and that matters just as much. Inevitably, some parts of your presentation are going to be less exciting. That's okay. The trick is to make sure that those less exciting parts (logistics, legal, whatever else) don't last too long and don't come too close together. Plotting your pitch lets you continually switch up the emotional tenor of the presentation to make sure that your audience *doesn't* slip into autopilot.

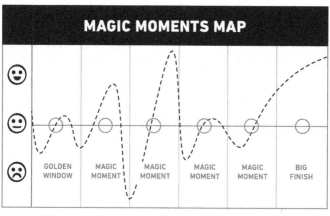

MAGIC MOMENTS MAP

BEGINNING   MIDDLE   END

DEFINITIONS:

The **Golden Window** is the first 30 seconds of your presentation. It's when you have the greatest amount of the audience's attention. And if you don't do something interesting or unexpected in that window, you'll start to lose them.

Magic moments force the customer to disengage their autopilot system and give you their full attention. There are 5 ways to create these moments in your pitch:

M - make it surprising
A - analyze them on a deeper level
G - give the pitch in the right order
I - include 3D objects
C - co-create together

The **peak-end rule** states that individuals base their opinion of an experience not on the full event, but on (1) the most emotionally intense part (whether good or bad) and (2) the end. So make sure that the end is memorable and leaves them feeling great.

DOWNLOAD THIS POSTER AND OTHER BONUS GIFTS AT GOBIGBONUS.COM

Case Study: How Knapheide Went All-In to Give Clients and Distributors One Unforgettable Experience

"On paper," Bo Knapheide admits, "our sales experience program doesn't make sense." Bo is the CEO and President of Knapheide, a 175-year-old maker of work truck bodies and truck beds, and the sales experience program he's talking about would give most corporate accountants hives. A significant portion of the company's marketing budget is dedicated to two private jets. But they're not for the executives. They're for clients and distributors. "Most companies," says Bo, "use planes to go out. We use planes to bring people in."

Despite having been a family company for six generations, Knapheide has a marketing problem. It's located in the middle of absolutely nowhere. Quincy, Illinois is a small rural town over two hours from the nearest major airport. For some companies, this isn't a huge problem, but Knapheide's business depends enormously on trust—trust that the product is solid, that it will handle anything a day in the life of a working truck can throw at it. The best way to build that trust is for clients to see with their own eyes how Knapheide builds its products to last. But asking potential clients to fly out to them, then rent a car and drive is a nonstarter. So about thirty years ago, Bo's father just went ahead and bought a jet.

Today, up to five days a week, the Knapheide planes jet across the United States, bring people to Quincy, give them a tour of the factory, then have them home in time for supper. Knapheide doesn't just invite their customers either. They also bring in their distributors (they have over 250, as far away as Alaska, who install the custom mounts that Knapheide manufactures), who can in turn bring their clients and forge lasting bonds with *them*. The vast majority of their passengers have never been on a private jet before, so it's an extraordinary experience from the very moment their car drives onto the tarmac.

From that point forward, the tour is full of small magic moments. For instance, a local artist (who's been doing this for thirty years) makes a customized painting for every single guest. It's the first thing the guest sees when they walk through the doors of the plant, and then they take it home with them and hang it in their offices. "I've had competitors tell me they've walked into people's offices, seen those prints, and just say, 'Well, hell, this is done.'"

According to Bo, "My father always said, 'Good companies have a soul.' Bringing people in to see us lets them understand that soul. It lets us back up everything we say. From a distance, all the 'family company' culture stuff might seem like just a sales pitch. But when you're here, it becomes real. You can *see* our guests change their demeanor throughout the day."

Bo says visitors often start off tight-lipped or with their arms crossed—they know they're being pitched, and they don't *want* to be wowed by the big flashy plane; they're here about trucks, not planes. But as the day goes on, they run through a series of smaller, quieter experiences as they visit with Knapheide's people, learn the history, eat the local cheese soup, and the emotional connections begin to build. Because that's the thing about an emotional connection—it's involuntary. Those magic moments make your prospects a lot more likely to listen and remember every moment of the experience. And they also make them more likely to buy.

Bo summarized the effect: "On a typical business call, it's like 'Okay, I've got an hour. Let's get this done.' But when you have a whole day, the way people open up is pretty special. It lets us show exactly who we are, and they get to do the same. By showing everything you've got, you establish trust. When you say goodbye, you get a completely different reaction than when you said hello."

We're not suggesting that you go out and buy a Gulfstream. Although this approach works for Knapheide, "expensive" isn't the same thing as memorable. The next five chapters offer a menu of tools to spark these magic moments—and more importantly, we show you how to use them on any budget, large or small. Whether you have a really important customer you want to go all out to impress or you want to review the way your sales team engages with every prospect, each chapter will offer you a different way to give them a pitch they'll never forget.

CHAPTER 3

MAKE IT
SURPRISING

MAKE IT SURPRISING

ANALYZE THEM ON A DEEPER LEVEL

GIVE THE PITCH IN THE RIGHT ORDER

INCLUDE 3D OBJECTS

CO-CREATE TOGETHER

There is a bouncer in the brain of every person you will ever pitch to. It's called the reticular activating system, or RAS.

Every second, your brain receives approximately 11 million bits of data. The conscious mind, however, can process only 40–50 bits per second.[12] The RAS figures out which bits get in, and keeps everything else out.

Your RAS is important. Marketers today estimate that in 2022, the average person saw 10,000 advertisements per day, up from 5,000 a day in 2007.[13] Your brain needs to avoid almost all of those pulls for attention or you won't be able to function, let alone get anything accomplished at work. But once something gets through, your brain's RAS will assume it's important and keep showing you information just like it. For instance, say you buy a Subaru. Immediately, you'll start noticing way more Subarus on the road. There has not been a huge surge of people buying Subarus. This effect is your RAS saying, *Hey, you're interested in this thing, right? Here's more of it.* Those Subarus have always been there; you've just never been conscious of them.

As individuals trying to land an initial meeting or an opportunity, our first challenge is getting past the RAS to convince the prospect to pay attention. No matter how many times you've tried to contact them, they likely may not have even realized that they've received the solicitation. It's in a huge pile of 9,900 other solicitations that they didn't even see that day, thanks to the RAS.

So how do we get through the RAS? We use the Go Big or Go Home method to elicit surprise and emotion before we even meet them!

Case Study: How Diana Got into an Exclusive Business Accelerator by Using Stalk and Awe

In 2008, at the age of twenty-seven, Diana launched her first startup, a company that helped businesses find and manage their lawyers. The business made $70,000 in its first year and Diana was trying to figure out the best way to grow it. Then, one day, she read an article that said a large foundation was starting a business accelerator right there in Kansas City for, specifically, tech companies that wanted to scale from zero to $100 million in only three years. Diana's company fit exactly none of those criteria, but she instinctively knew that whatever mentoring and educational opportunities they were offering would significantly help her business. She had to try to get in.

The article listed the head of the program as a successful entrepreneur named Bo Fishback. Diana excitedly called

Bo at the foundation and left a message. No response. Next, she figured out Bo's email and wrote to him. Nothing. She politely emailed him again, just to ask for a meeting. Nothing.

Undeterred, Diana and her husband, Jason, opened up their LinkedIn profiles. It turned out they knew only one person who worked at the foundation. That wasn't enough. So they searched for any individuals who *did* have contacts there. Diana and Jason called twenty of the people on that list and asked them to call their friend at the foundation and ask them to "tell Bo Fishback to meet with Diana Kander."

It was a complex game of telephone but totally worth the effort. Diana had no idea if these people were actually making the calls. After a week, she emailed Bo again. This time, he agreed to meet for lunch.

Diana stood by the hostess stand, waiting for Bo at the restaurant. She distinctly remembers him marching through the front door and looming over her with his six-foot-seven frame. "Who *are* you?" he said, with a huge smile on his face. "All week, people have been coming up to me to tell me to meet with you! They're still coming up to me! I'm having to tell everyone, *yes, I'm meeting with her.*"

Diana got into the program. The first year in the program, her company grew to over $800,000 in revenue—an increase of over 1000 percent. Most importantly, she's still friends with Bo.

Diana calls this move the Stalk and Awe. To be clear, the stalking is professional. Don't do anything untoward or illegal. But that initial overwhelming delight can create strong emotional peaks, ones that make the rest of the pitch less of an uphill battle.

The Stalk and Awe may not be the best approach for every situation. And maybe it doesn't feel natural to you. But there is still a way you can grab somebody's attention in a memorable way. It involves showing them how important they are to you and that you aren't interested in a tired, transactional relationship.

**The key is to invest in them
before they invest in you.**

Case Study: How an Event Planning Company Grew Its Business 250 Percent during COVID-19

Joan Wells is the epitome of what you can do when your clients trust you. As events all over the country began to vanish as a result of COVID-19 in 2020, she was still able to grow her meetings and events agency, Wellington, 250 percent over the next two years.

Joan has a unique approach to marketing her services. It's a core value she'll share at her first meeting with a prospect: *We invest in you before you invest in us.*

What does it mean to "invest"? Wells and her team will fly out to meet with you for that first meeting, regardless of whether or not you have an immediate need for her business. They will bring you a unique gift, share a meal if possible, ask about your business, and above all, they will say *almost nothing about their services* unless you ask.

If you think this sounds crazy, you're not alone. "People are always shocked," says Wells, "because we're willing to invest in coming out to meet with them. At first, they want us to know they can't promise us anything, and that's when we let them know that this is one of our core values."

Wells's goal isn't to close a deal; it's to create a relationship where none existed before. What's especially effective is that often, the clients naturally assume that there must be *some* agenda here, some stealth pitch coming at the end. So when, instead, the entire conversation is about the prospect, who they are, and what they want to create, it feels like a breath of fresh air. And at the end, says Wells, the potential client often says, *Gosh, it was so great getting to know all about your company.* It doesn't matter that Wells didn't talk much about her company. They feel an emotional connection—the kind that allows us to *feel* like we know someone, even when we don't.

This approach hasn't just been successful for Wellington in the short run; it's proved durable. Wells says that her team looked at a list of their largest clients over the last twenty years and realized that "every single one of them started with one of these introductory conversations rather than with an RFP." More importantly, these kinds of personal meetings help *keep* clients.

In 2000, Wellington's biggest client was a big three automaker. One day, Wells got a letter that explained that the automaker had reviewed all of their 150+ event vendors and had decided to consolidate their business down to a list of three—and Wellington wasn't on the list. "The problem, we realized, was that here was an executive who had never met us, who didn't know how we worked." So Wellington contacted all the execs at the automaker who *had* worked with her firm, asking them to write letters testifying to their relationship. Then Wells called the executive in charge and asked to fly out to see him. He was dubious, but the very next week, Wells was in his office, giving a presentation of the impact she had already made in their organization. Wellington was added to the list of vendors who stayed. And today, that list is down to two, with Wellington still on it.

What it all adds up to is that essential ingredient: trust. "It's like being the first person to say, 'I love you,'" she jokes. The client understands that by investing in them, Wells is *trusting* that they're not going to abuse that investment by, say, asking for free advice and then using her suggestions without hiring her. **Investing in them shows that you're interested in a relationship and not just the sale.**

Thus, when almost all of the events on their books started canceling in the first quarter of 2020, Wells and her team started reaching out to people across the country for virtual coffees, building new relationships and strengthening existing ones. Despite the total shutdown of in-person events, Wellington actually grew modestly in 2020. And in 2021, they exploded, growing 250 percent, even as COVID-19 waves continued to crash around the country. The same year, they were acquired by Augeo, where Wells is now President of Experience.[14]

Of course, not everyone can fly all over the country arranging meetings with no expectations. And in the B2B setting, where pitches often have to be made to committees and can have a staid, predictable feel, it can be hard to produce the kind of spontaneity necessary to generate an emotional connection. That's where the element of surprise comes in. Surprise, according to Tania Luna and Leeann Renninger, authors of *Surprise: Embrace the Unpredictable and Engineer the Unexpected*, "intensifies our emotions by about 400 percent," which is why good surprises feel so extraordinary, and bad surprises can leave us feeling so devastated and helpless.

Surprise also has an uncanny power to focus our attention. According to Luna and Renninger, being surprised freezes our neural function for 1/25th of a second—imperceptible in real time but an eternity in brain time. In that moment, the brain triggers an impulse that they call "find," which means that it floods with curiosity, trying to figure out what this new stimulus is all about.

When you walk into DI for the first time, you walk through a glass door into a vestibule, taking stock of the place—from the outside, it's an unassuming building. You see another glass door in front of you that leads into the building and what appears to be the welcome desk. And as you're making your way to that second door, you almost miss it. There, on the wall connecting the two doors under the word WELCOME is your name in big shiny metal letters. It almost looks permanent.

You stare at it for a second. You might even take a picture. And your entire disposition changes. You walk into the building with a smile on your face, curious at what other surprises await.

Surprising potential clients (and, just as crucially, existing ones) is basically a shortcut to their emotions. There are many ways to surprise a person, but the best surprises always happen during a moment they didn't expect.

John Ruhlin might be America's foremost expert at surprising business prospects and clients with gifts, which he calls Love Bombs. John is the founder and CEO of Giftology, and at his core, he treats the art of giving gifts much the same way Joan Wells approaches meeting people where they are. The goal is to create long-term relationships.

As Ruhlin says, it's all about expectations. The moment we're told that something is going to happen, our brains start projecting images of how it's going to happen. Maybe we're excited about the thing, so we get our hopes up, but once that happens, it's almost impossible to do anything but meet our expectations—forget exceeding them.

Think about Valentine's Day. Your spouse might reasonably expect that you will book a reservation at a nice restaurant (which will be filled with other couples) and maybe buy chocolate and flowers. These will all be described as "nice." But in recorded history, no one's mind has ever been blown by chocolates and a dinner on Valentine's Day because all you're doing is meeting expectations. You can screw up Valentine's Day, but you can't really *win* it.

Now imagine that you do something similar for your spouse, but now it's completely at random: they leave the office and you're standing there outside, holding flowers. You say the magic words: "The kids are with a babysitter. Get in the car." You drive to a restaurant, there's a reservation, you enjoy a nice dinner, and then surprise your spouse with a box of their favorite dessert. Think of how much more romantic voltage that meal has—all thanks to the element of surprise.

It's easy to surprise and delight people when there's no expectation. And there is very little expectation before a pitch. They don't even know you yet. That's why it's the best moment to show them some love.

"A gift is just a delivery vehicle
for an emotional connection."
—JOHN RUHLIN

When giving gifts, just don't fall into one of the biggest mistakes companies make: They go too cheap, and they make it all about *them*. To Ruhlin, there's nothing worse than the "trinketty swag" most companies dole out, like mugs and sweatshirts stamped with their logo. "Understand," he says, "that nobody cares about your brand or your logo; they care about *their* brand, their values."

John is the epitome of the Go Big or Go Home method. He has a great story about landing a meeting with the Executive Vice President of Sales for Aflac by gifting first and asking for the meeting second. John mailed a customized set of Cutco knives, one piece at a time for eight straight weeks. The first package was the knife block and a chef's knife with Aflac's logo, the executive's name, and his wife's name and a handwritten note that read, "Carve out five minutes for me." For the next seven weeks, John filled out the knife block with the full set, and after the last knife was delivered, John sent an email asking for a meeting. The executive wrote him back and said, "My wife loves you! You blew me away!" and was willing to give John whatever time he needed to make his pitch.

John believes that **if you're giving a gift to a very important prospect, you should give them something that shows the importance of the relationship.**

DI often uses gift-giving as part of their LTF pitches. Possibly their favorite gift of all time might also have been their smallest. The then-owner of the Miami Marlins, Jeffrey Loria, was an obsessive collector of bobblehead dolls. He wanted to create a bobblehead museum in the new Marlins stadium, and the architect of the project reached out to DI, explained the plan and the budgets, and asked for a proposal.

As soon as they started brainstorming, someone had the thought: What if they could design a display that would make the bobbleheads bobble all the time? After all, what a terrible fate for a bobblehead to just be parked in a glass case, its giant head frozen forevermore? Then someone came up with the idea of making it interactive by involving a touchscreen so that visitors could tell who each bobblehead represented because not all of them were immediately recognizable. The ideas were great—and way over the budget. But the DI team was so excited that they decided to put together the presentation anyhow.

The architect said they couldn't get an audience with Loria. So DI built a really cool box to package the proposal, which included a bobblehead of Jeffrey Loria. A few days after the box was shipped, it was returned with a post-it note from Loria's executive assistant. It read: "You should darken the gray hair."

DI followed the kind advice and sent the bobblehead back. A week later, the team lead was standing in an airport waiting for a flight when his phone rang with an unrecognized Miami number. It was Jeffrey Loria himself. "Okay," he said, "you got me. You win."

How you do anything is how you do everything.

Whether it's a personalized knife set or a custom bob-blehead doll, the purpose of a gift should always be the same: to create trust. **And to do that, the gift must—*must*—be given with an open hand.** No strings attached. That's why Joan Wells insistence on meeting with people she knows can't hire her at the moment holds such power. If someone says, "I can't give you anything," and you reply, "I know, but I care about you anyhow," it erases the usual transactional feel of these meetings, and they can let their guard down. The crowning value of a gift is that it shows clearly just how much you're willing to invest in them before they invest in you—or, if you're handing out cheap branded beer koozies, how little.

There is so much money at stake and so many people involved in the world of B2B sales that it can be easy for them to feel cold and generic. Clients can see those of us who pitch as manipulators that they have to be weary of, making it very hard to establish a personal connection. They don't *want* to be sold to. But with the Love Bombs or the no-stakes meetings, they don't just respond; they pick up the phone and call the salesperson who sent it, delighted. The sheer, uncomplicated surprise of the gift makes them feel seen as people and, in turn, lets them see the sender as a person, too.

CHAPTER 4

ANALYZE THEM ON A DEEPER LEVEL

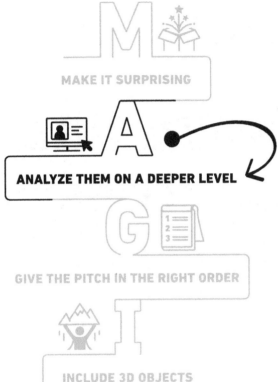

MAKE IT SURPRISING

ANALYZE THEM ON A DEEPER LEVEL

GIVE THE PITCH IN THE RIGHT ORDER

INCLUDE 3D OBJECTS

CO-CREATE TOGETHER

Avoid the "One of Three Problem"

CEB Global defined the One of Three Problem as what happens when customers do their own research and narrow down the available options to three acceptable providers that they know will deliver business value.[15] Then the customer kicks off a bidding war that gets them the lowest possible price, turning each of the top three firms into mere commodities. Once this customer has decided that price is their main concern, they become very hard to reach. If you want to avoid the One of Three Problem, you have to show your prospects that you understand them in a way none of the other vendors do. That you see life from their point of view. That you connect on this other level that's hard to even put into words.

> The only way to connect in a way that no one else can is to do research that no one else will.

Case Study: How United Airlines Chose a New Marketing Agency

In 2021, after a year of unprecedented upheaval in their industry, executives at United Airlines decided they wanted to hire a new advertising agency to create and purchase airtime for their commercials, so they put out an RFP to four ad companies. Right away, all four companies got to work doing their research. They logged hours on calls with United executives asking burning questions and pre-pitching ideas to make sure they were on the same page. They were doing exactly what they were supposed to, pressure-testing their messages.

According to Josh Earnest, Chief Communications Officer of United, one of the most impressive pitches came from a hot, buzzy boutique agency in New York with a flashy office overlooking a helipad on the East River. They were well-schooled in the art of projecting confidence and competence. They even had a balcony with a gorgeous view of Lower Manhattan. Like the other companies, they'd been in close contact with United in the lead-up to the pitch. In their presentation, says Earnest, "their approach was, 'we've won all of these big awards and have a lot of big-name clients, and we're going to knock your socks off with all our creative horsepower.'" The agency went all out to show the clients how talented and original they were—and they succeeded. "They were super smart," says Earnest. "They had creative ideas and they put a lot of effort into it."

It was, in other words, a compelling argument. And if all the other firms had made similarly compelling arguments, they might have won. But one small LA-based agency called 72andSunny did a different kind of research to understand the culture of the company they were pitching.

"They were definitely not the biggest company," says Earnest, "and they weren't the frontrunner." But they'd done something no one else had. Although all the companies had been in consistent contact with the United execs who would be making the decision, 72andSunny asked United to give them access to employees. Their team wound up spending an entire day at LAX trailing and interviewing frontline workers, asking questions, and trying to understand their duties and challenges.

"What that firsthand experience gave them was a really good granular feel of our business that came through in the presentation," says Earnest. He even admits that neither he nor his team could exactly put their fingers on *why* 72andSunny's presentation was so much better than anyone else's. It wasn't that there was one perfect mic-drop sentence or showstopping image. And it wasn't like they got "extra credit" for having spent the day at LAX. It was just that the United team felt so much more *understood* by 72andSunny's pitch. "They just had a more nuanced, sophisticated, richer picture of the company," says Earnest.

For example, before the presentation began, 72andSunny gave out copies of a twenty-page mini magazine all about the people who worked at LAX. They'd designed and printed it themselves, and they made it clear that whether or not they won the account, they wanted Earnest and his team to have it so that they could feel more connected to their own people.

Moreover, by designing a marketing strategy that was based on what employees had shared, they'd wound up giving United the thing it really wanted: an advertising campaign that would also speak to their employees, who had been relentlessly battered by a year of furloughs, health anxiety, mask enforcement, and a frightening spike in unruly passengers. Much of this advertising was going to be in airports—and "who spends more time in an airport than airline employees?"

It didn't matter that the United team couldn't say exactly why 72andSunny's pitch was better. "It was like, 'you know it when you see it,'" says Earnest. In the end, the decision was unanimous. What Earnest is describing is communication that connected with the subconscious minds of the United Airlines team. It gave them the feeling of "just right" that a well-executed emotional experience is supposed to. And it all stemmed from the immersive research 72andSunny invested in.

How to Research Individuals

What if you're not pitching a selection committee? What if you're pitching just one millionaire or senior executive to close the deal? Your basic prospect research isn't going to help you create any magic moments. You've got to understand them on a deeper level and figure out what matters to them personally. That's because B2B purchasers are almost 50 percent more likely to buy a product or service when they see personal benefit to themselves, like an opportunity to advance their careers or merely to feel confidence or pride in their purchase decision.[16] And they are *eight* times more likely to pay a premium on a product or service when they believe personal value is present.

Psychographic research is how you understand your customers on that deeper level, uncovering their values, desires, goals, and interests. This type of research will allow you to communicate in a way that triggers emotional peaks and conveys that personal value. It arms you with a keen sense of *their* needs—and what solution might be the right fit.

Once you understand just how far people who follow the Go Big or Go Home method will go to understand the subconscious of their potential clients, you'll see how essential it is to put this kind of research at the core of your pitching strategy.

How Trial Lawyers Do It

Imagine you're a lawyer going to trial. Before you get to make your case, you go through the jury selection process, where your job is to narrow thirty-six total strangers down to twelve—and those twelve have the fate of your client (and your bank account) in their hands. So how do you pick? Sure, you can ask them questions. But which questions should you even ask?

One of the things you can do is hire a jury consultant like Kevin Boully, an expert on using public records and social media searches to profile potential jurors (or judges or arbitrators) for law firms. From the moment the full jury pool files into the room and their names are given to the legal teams, Kevin goes to work in his office working up psychographic profiles of each individual juror.

It doesn't take long, he says—sometimes all it takes is a five-minute stroll through a juror's Twitter profile—but the trick is knowing how to look. Even if people aren't spouting off about their opinions online, social media can tell you where people like to vacation and what kind of culture they like. Public records searches using databases like LexisNexis can tell you the value of their house, their family members, or if they've been arrested. These are the same records that journalists use to pull up contact information for potential sources. Political organizations also use them to create donor profiles for prospects they are targeting.

This isn't the dark arts or anything invasive. From a lawyer's standpoint, understanding the value systems and backgrounds of jurors doesn't just help detect potential bias during the selection process; it also helps guide lawyers in crafting arguments that will build intimacy between their client and the jury. And in business, understanding the people you're pitching makes the relationships you build stronger, and more fruitful for all parties involved.

Whether you're going to trial or pitching a project, your goal is to find ways to persuade someone else to take your side. **The point is to create a more three-dimensional profile of a prospect so that you're pitching a real person as opposed to a human-shaped wallet.**

We figured the easiest way to show you how to collect and deploy psychographic research was to do it on ourselves. So we asked Cameron Sullivan, who creates these kinds of three-dimensional profiles for business and donor pitches, to create one on each of us. Rather than provide typical author bios at the end of the book, which are usually just narrative versions of a résumé, we included Cameron's profiles instead, along with all the sources he used. You can find them in the Appendix. Our hope is that these examples will help you see how much easier it would be to create an instant connection with a prospect, start the conversation off with a thoughtful question, and tailor whatever you are selling to how they see the world.

But you don't need to hire Cameron to get a psychographic understanding of your prospect. All you need to do is invest the time to get to know them. We're so used to understanding our customer's demographics: size of company, position, tenure, age, education level, etc. It's like looking at a resume. But as anyone with experience hiring people knows, a resume never tells the whole story.

Demographics only explain who the buyer is. Psychographic research explains why they buy.

Case Study: Creating a Go Big or Go Home Pitch to Land a Job

Diana's friend Sarah was desperate. She was a digital marketer for a company in the Midwest, but she was miserable. The culture was toxic and they refused to pay her any more than $50,000, even though she was responsible for generating a large part of their sales. Sarah tried to leave, but she had a run of bad luck where she'd apply for positions and either hear nothing or get an interview and then wind up not getting the job. Diana shared an online posting with her for a position that looked like a dream job at a dream company, but Sarah was intimidated: because of her job-hunting experience up to this point, she was worried that she wouldn't get far in the interview process.

At Diana's urging, she applied anyway. She not only got an interview but made it through several rounds until the company was down to three finalists. Sarah asked Diana to work with her to figure out how she could stand out from the competition, and Diana realized that this would be a great test case for the Go Big or Go Home hypothesis. Together they set about trying to brainstorm a way to create a magic moment.

Sarah learned that the CEO of this company had made several YouTube videos of himself giving presentations, as well as posted short articles on LinkedIn to share his views on company culture and innovation. Few people had seen these, but it was clear that he wanted to develop a presence as a thought leader and keynote speaker. Fortunately, in a previous life, Sarah had experience creating websites and materials for speakers (like Diana), so she was able to deploy her skills to make a mock webpage advertising the CEO as a public speaker. She used the videos and articles he'd posted online as key topics and matched the design of the page to the exact look and feel of the company's existing website. It took her just a few hours.

The final interview was over Zoom, and it began with the usual formalities. The decision makers, including the CEO, asked her their questions, and she answered them confidently.

And as the conversation was winding down, she asked, "Before we wrap up, do you all mind if I share my screen? I want to show you something. I was so excited by this opportunity that I just couldn't help myself and I had to make this site. You're free to use it whether you hire me or not."

With the touch of a button, the Zoom window revealed the website Sarah had built. Instantly, the CEO saw not only the very thing he'd wanted brought to life, but he and everyone else also saw how perfectly Sarah would fit into their company. It was as if she already worked for them, and the only thing left was some paperwork.

After the interview, her point of contact emailed with only one question: "Would $100,000 be enough?"

CHAPTER 5

GIVE THE PITCH IN THE RIGHT ORDER

MAKE IT SURPRISING

ANALYZE THEM ON A DEEPER LEVEL

GIVE THE PITCH IN THE RIGHT ORDER

INCLUDE 3D OBJECTS

CO-CREATE TOGETHER

Our Natural Instincts Lead Us to Pitch Backward

Think for a minute about how you usually pitch prospects. The order of your presentation probably involves introducing yourself, discussing the value of your product or service, and then concluding with why they should buy. It makes sense: you start by talking about yourself because you want the prospect to have a clear sense of who you are. The more they understand who you are and how your company works, the more likely they are to hire you. But this is completely backward.

> **They don't care about your story until they believe that you understand their story.**

Case Study: How FBI Hostage Negotiator Chris Voss Learned to Gain Trust Quickly[17]

Chris Voss was the FBI's chief international hostage and kidnapping negotiator from 2003 to 2007. Because he was dealing with cases in wildly different corners of the globe, places where he didn't speak the language, he often had two separate negotiation challenges. First, the obvious one: dealing with the kidnappers or hostage takers. But the second challenge was almost as complex: convincing the families of the hostages to let him do his job.

One time, Voss was on the case of a twelve-year-old boy who was kidnapped in Haiti. The boy was an American citizen, so the FBI had jurisdiction, but Voss still had to convince the father to let him lead the negotiation strategy. And the father was more than skeptical. "You're in Washington, DC," he said. "How *you* gonna help *me*?"

Voss knew that he had just seconds to make a first impression before this guy hung up the phone. Seconds to tell a desperate father how he could help and win this man's trust.

Voss knew from past experience that the way most people pitch is flawed. In the past, he started out these kinds of conversations by boasting about his experience with the FBI, explaining that he basically wrote the FBI's manual for hostage negotiations. "They might as well have yawned in my face," says Voss.

He learned that focusing on logic and reason won't get you far in establishing trust over a short period of time. **"Your résumé correlates *loosely* with whether or not you know what you're doing,"** he says. And we all know it! Credentials are meaningless in a crisis. **Reciting your experience is not a way to build trust; *showing* it is.** That father was in the grip of a storm of terrible emotions. His son had been taken. He was helpless, angry, confused, and most of all, scared to death. In this emotional state, people have no patience, no time for politeness, and they absolutely don't care about your CV. He needed Voss to *prove*, right then and there, that he *would* free his son.

So what *did* Voss say to this man he'd never met and couldn't see?

"All right, so Haitian kidnappers are not killing kidnap victims these days. I realize that's really stupid because they kill each other at the drop of a hat, but they're *not* killing kidnap victims. Now today is Thursday, and Haitian kidnappers love to party on Saturday night. So if you say the things that I want you to say, when I want you to say them, we'll have your son out late Friday, early Saturday morning."

The father didn't skip a beat. "Tell me what you want me to do," he said.

Why was Voss's response so powerful? Because he knew that what the father was really asking was the same question companies are asking when you pitch them: *Do you see what I see? Do you know what I'm looking at?* The father never asked how long Chris had been with the FBI, or how long he'd been a negotiator, or how many people he'd freed. He didn't ask how often he'd been to Haiti (never) or if he spoke French or Creole (he only speaks English). **Customers ask for that kind of information only when we fail to *demonstrate* our ability to see what they are up against.**

The boy was released on early Saturday morning.

Understand the Danger of Storytelling

We love to start a meeting by sharing a story about ourselves.

It's hard to not talk about ourselves, because doing so is like a drug to our brain. Talking about our likes, our dislikes, and our life experiences lights up the same parts of our brain as sex, cocaine, and sugar.[18] It makes our brain release dopamine, which is why sometimes, when we start talking about ourselves, we can't stop, *even when we know we should.*

When we're seeking to impress someone—on a date, at a party, in a pitch—we usually resort to storytelling, and usually those stories are about us. To quote the English philosopher William Hazlitt, "We talk little when we do not talk about ourselves."

It's a natural human instinct: when we want someone to like us, we offer stories that depict us in our best or most charming moments. That instinct prevails across virtually all human interaction, including business pitches.

That's why the lawyers in Diana's story and the New York ad agency in Josh Earnest's story felt so good after their presentations—they'd been talking about themselves. **If you judge the success of a pitch based on how good *you* feel afterward, there's a high likelihood that you're being suckered by that dopamine surge.** Because as good as it makes you feel, it does absolutely nothing for your prospects.

The reason why working to *impress* potential clients is so doomed to failure is that you're a salesperson and they're naturally suspicious of you. They know you're giving them the rosiest projections of your features, benefits, customer loyalty, or whatever else. If you can't put that suspicion to bed, nothing you say is going to stick in their minds.

Stop trying to impress your clients and start focusing on creating a connection.

That way, they'll be receptive to the magic moments you've got planned. The key is to think more about *their* story than yours.

When Joan Wells kicks off her meetings with the people she's flown in to talk to, she doesn't start by saying, "Let me tell you a little about us." Instead, she comes armed with a thought-provoking question. If it's truly a cold meeting, with no real advance engagement, the question will be something simple like, "What's the biggest challenge your organization faces?" But if there's some relationship there already, she'll go bigger: "What is one thing that occurred in your life that is the reason you're sitting here today?"

Either way, says Wells, these questions instantly transform the vibe in the room. The atmosphere ceases to be pitchy. Now it's collaborative, even emotional. The answers, in turn, are a gold mine of information for Wells's team. When people speak about the thing that led them to this place, they're telling her *their* story and what they care about. From that point forward, Wells can speak directly to individuals in the room: "As Jessica said," or "Going back to Robert's story." It makes everyone in the room feel seen and understood. Moreover, it gives each person that very dopamine hit that generally the person pitching hoards for themselves.

Case Study: How Mark Cuban Used Nostalgia to Sell Mavericks Tickets[19]

In 2000, Mark Cuban bought the Dallas Mavericks for $285 million. There are two interesting things about this sale. First, he bought it from H. Ross Perot Jr., son of the Texas billionaire-cum-presidential candidate. Second, at that point the Mavericks had been voted the worst franchise in professional sports. They were chronically dysfunctional and had only won 40 percent of their games over the last two *decades*. They'd rarely made the playoffs, and attendance was abysmal. Fans were justifiably furious.

Cuban's first and most important job was to get fans to start buying tickets to the games again, but it's hard to sell people on bringing their kids to games the team is probably going to lose. Kids take this stuff hard. Heck, grown-ups take losing hard. So Cuban did something few team owners ever do: inserted himself right into the heart of the operation and started calling previous season ticket holders who'd had it with the endless losing and canceled their subscriptions. "I didn't even have an office," he says.

"There was a sales bullpen…and I put my desk right in the middle of it…I had a laptop and a phonebook and I started calling people…Because I wasn't going to ask somebody else to start making calls if I wouldn't."

First of all, no one had ever heard of an owner calling fans personally—owners were supposed to be aloof, distant, and sometimes eccentric, but they weren't supposed to concern themselves with such petty matters as individual ticket holders. And second, remember that in 2000 basically no one had heard of Mark Cuban. He wasn't the *Shark Tank* celebrity he is now; he was just another dot-com guy who'd sold his business to Yahoo! So if a guy named Mark Cuban called you out of the blue, even if you knew who he was, you'd have a right to be skeptical.

Just like Chris Voss, Cuban knew he had an extremely brief window in which to make a good impression and get his listener's buy-in. So how did he do it? What story could he tell in thirty seconds that would overcome the skepticism and bring them back to the arena?

Think for a second. What would you do?

Say you tried to introduce yourself to them, to let them get to know you. After all, you just bought this franchise—you're the public face of it. If they can relate to you, then maybe they'll understand that someone like-minded is finally running things.

Or more likely, they'll listen to you politely and then hang up, because you've made the mistake of thinking they care about you. They don't. They especially can't relate to you—you're a bazillionaire who just bought their team. You're just trying to sell them something.

Okay, so don't talk about you. Tell the caller all about how much you're plowing into this team, all the big acquisitions you're going to make, all your plans for greatness. Maybe if you can make them believe in the team again, they'll come back.

They won't. They've heard promises like this before; they're not interested in what you're *going* to do, and moreover, they've been burned so many times that they're not going to get fooled again.

In both these pitches, note that the goal is to convince the ticketholder of something, to *change* their mind. And that's a really tall order. **You can't change their mind with logic. But if you can trigger an emotional response, their gut feelings will overpower their objections.** Which is exactly what Mark Cuban did when they picked up the phone. Here's what he said:

> Hi, this is Mark Cuban, new owner of the Dallas Mavericks. I know you've been to a game, and I just wanted to sit here and tell you that I would love to have you back. Did you know that going to a Mavs game is less expensive than eating at McDonald's? Did you know that we have tickets now that are less expensive than going to the movies? And you'll get a unique experience that you'll never ever experience anywhere else.

Then he would give the person on the other end a chance to respond. Imagine your beloved sports franchise is a dumpster fire that's been blazing for twenty years, and out of the blue, the new owner calls you. You'd probably use that opportunity to give them a piece of your mind. The word "sucks" would probably get a lot of use—and for Cuban, it did. Cuban didn't argue, though. He didn't say, "I'm turning things around." He didn't make promises. Instead, he said:

> Do you remember when your mom or dad took you to your first Mavs game? [Pause for response] Do you remember how you felt? [Pause for response]. Do you get that going to McDonald's? Do you get that going to the movies? No. We create special experiences. I can't guarantee you we are going to win or lose, but I can guarantee you we're going to provide the entertainment. And when you look at your son or daughter's face, you will be thrilled to death and know that you can't get that experience anywhere else. And it's eight dollars a ticket.

He didn't try to change their mind about the prospects for the Mavericks; he tried to remind them how they *used* to feel going to a Mavericks game and how they wanted to feel again. The emotional connection was already there; Cuban was just reactivating it. Here, after a parade of useless owners who were using their team as a front for real estate speculation was an owner who actually *understood* why basketball meant something to them. And then he was putting an incredibly low dollar amount on it. Cuban, for his part, understood that he wasn't selling basketball. He was selling an emotional experience. And by promising to give fans a chance to re-experience that feeling that made them season ticket-holders once before, through the eyes of their children, he was giving them an opportunity for something truly special. And he was giving them a terrific deal on it to boot. From 2001 through 2020, the Mavericks sold out over 800 consecutive games, the longest sellout streak in major American sports history.[20]

We're not saying you can't *ever* speak about yourself. If you have competitors who are similar to you and your overall marketing approach is similar to theirs, it's of course important to differentiate your company in your pitch. And once you've forged a connection with the client by uncovering their story, they will likely *want* to know more about yours. **Once they want to say yes, they'll want to know who they're saying yes to.** And how you choose to tell that "story" can make all the difference.

Imagine if after his phone pitch, Mark Cuban had said, "Now let me tell you a little bit about me" and proceeded to recite his résumé. The emotional peak of his pitch would have been forgotten, washed away by the wave of boredom.

Unfortunately, this is exactly how most B2B pitches share their origin story: they tell stories that aren't really stories.

> **Storytelling may be a natural instinct,
> but that doesn't mean that it comes naturally.**

There's nothing more boring than a person who can't tell a good story. Unfortunately, most business stories are built as educational parables. By overvaluing efficiency and "the takeaway," they commit one of the gravest crimes against storytelling: they're all about the destination and treat the journey as an inconvenience.

But the journey is the thing that grabs listeners, makes them sit forward in their seats. The journey is how we grow attached to the characters so that when something happens to them, we actually *care*. If that essential process hasn't happened, then the climax will be met with indifference, no matter how big the budget.

Case Study: How Clay Alexander Closed a Giant Deal with Cardinal Health to Distribute Lifesaving Cures

Clay Alexander is a master of the Go Big or Go Home method. This book could have easily included a different Clay story in every chapter. From selling his own lightbulb to GE (to repeat: he sold a *lightbulb*. To *GE*), to partnering with Starbucks to sell his self-heating coffee mug, the Ember—the first consumer electronic product ever sold by Starbucks—Clay is a surgeon with every emotional tool in this book. He's even got a whole pre-pitch preparation ritual to make sure he's at his physical peak when he goes in the room. But when he had to pitch Cardinal Health on the biggest opportunity he'd ever been involved with, even Clay had his work cut out for him.

Clay had used Ember's thermal control technology to invent a reusable self-refrigerating box that could be used to hold medicines or vaccines at a consistent temperature as they were shipped anywhere. The tech had the potential to revolutionize medical product shipping, which at the time relied on cardboard boxes, dry ice, and Styrofoam to move $20 billion worth of medicine around. But first, he had to convince the Cardinal Health executives. And on the morning of the pitch, all of his methodical prep went out the window when he awoke in Nashville to find his body covered in a poison ivy rash.

First, Clay rushed to the Rite-Aid and bought all the anti-itch cream he could find and mummified himself in bandages. Then he headed to the meeting where immediately he ran into another problem. "I'm used to like eight people being at a pitch meeting," he says. "I crush it in those intimate settings. And they walked us straight into this monster conference room with forty people sitting there staring at us. And I was like, 'Shit, okay, this is *not* an intimate setting.'"

Half-delirious with itching, Clay steeled himself and did the thing he does best: connect. He put his stuff down and started working the room, going up to every single person there and introducing himself, making small talk. Not only did this help them warm to him, he says, "it also helped me stop seeing them as an audience and start seeing them as people. Otherwise, it reminds you of being in elementary school when you are new in class, and you have to get up in front of all these people and introduce yourself."

When that was done, the pitch began in earnest. The first thing he did was engage the audience visually with a short, highly produced video highlighting the amazing technology and possibility of the box (more on the power of this in Chapter 6). Every element of the pitch was targeted to Cardinal specifically. "You never want someone to think you're going door to door," Clay says. He knew that Cardinal was committed to sustainability, so in the renderings, he put solar panels on the roof of their distribution center. He then went to the trouble of making sure that the center and even the delivery trucks all had an "Ember + Cardinal" logo on them. That took considerable time and expense, but people noticed—it was as if the partnership already existed and they were just here to hash out numbers.

Then, when Clay did start to talk about himself, he didn't share his résumé or his accomplishments. He shared his *why*.

Clay has told the origin story of Ember in every pitch he's ever been in, whether he's selling a self-warming baby bottle or a vaccine refrigeration box. He even puts a card telling the story into every Ember product's packaging. It's a simple story about being at breakfast with his family and his eggs going cold for the umpteenth time and thinking, *Why isn't there a solution for this?* Right there, he establishes himself as a **character**, one we can relate to, sure, but one whose ingenuity and resourcefulness amazes us. He tells the story of building the prototype out of RC car batteries, then figuring out the coffee mug and deciding he was going to sell this thing at Starbucks, even though Starbucks had never sold a consumer electronic product before. And now, he's introduced some **conflict**—there are stakes to this story now. He tells how he scrambled to get it into production in time for the holidays, and we start to experience the **journey**. Then, and only then, does he give the **resolution**: Starbucks agrees to sell it, they see monster sales, Ember winds up in every big-box store, and so on. And since it's about how much *Starbucks* made, this is also a story of customer success. Once he's told that story, Clay says, "People feel a connection to me and to the Ember brand."

So when you tell *your* story, don't race to the big finish. Focus on the spark, the thing that made you *need* to create this product or start this campaign. Give the clients a sense of how you and your company struggled and almost failed—but didn't. Give them a story they can *cheer* for. "We're all just humans here," says Clay, "and we all like stories. We all want to feel a bond with other people."

The power of the origin story is that it helps people see you as a human being and connect to you on an emotional level. Diana's been a keynote speaker on curiosity and innovation ever since she sold her legal consulting company in 2014, giving speeches to over 100,000 people. No matter the audience makeup, she frequently shares her origin story of escaping from the Soviet Union in the middle of the night when she was just seven years old. Her family spoke no English, had just over $200 to their name, and could take only one suitcase per person. They knew so little about where they were going or what was in store that one of the suitcases was one-third full of just toilet paper.

Diana didn't like growing up poor. She didn't like splitting an ice-cream cone four ways or looking for toys in the apartment complex dumpster. She was determined to change her fate, so she created a little formula for success: Figure out how things work to find the opportunities. And there are always opportunities.

At fourteen, she joined a multilevel marketing program and sold commercial water filters door to door. By her senior year of high school, in addition to waiting tables twenty hours a week, she was selling flea market goods to classmates at a markup, all to afford going to college. And to avoid paying full tuition, she finished a four-year degree in just two and a half years by finding every obscure way to earn college credits.

Agility and curiosity aren't just buzzwords to Diana—they are the vital skills that helped her survive and flourish in the United States.

Similarly, when Tucker gives talks, he frequently shares that when he was in second grade, his parents got divorced, and his mom and stepfather moved him and his sister to a very remote part of southern Missouri to live in a three-story teepee. The nearest town was twelve miles away and had fewer than 1,000 people. The closest telephone was a shared party line at Glady's house, which was a mile-and-a-half walk down the road. They didn't have electricity or normal running water, and they built the teepee themselves.

He explains that all of this allowed him space to sit under kerosene lamps—drawing, inventing things. His imagination ran wild because he had nothing else to do.

When Tucker makes a presentation and doesn't tell this story and there's someone in the audience who *has* heard it before, they often come up to him afterward to ask, "Why didn't you tell the teepee story?" They feel like something important is missing.

All three of these origin stories are effective because they have two main things in common: First, they help us create connection with the audience. Tucker's designs aren't just renderings; they're the evolution of the drawings a little boy did by the light of a kerosene lamp—and how can anyone fail to connect to that? And second, they are *entertaining*. Wherever we are and whatever we are doing, whether it's a pitch, a university lecture, or even a funeral, human beings want to be entertained. We want to laugh, to gasp, to be moved. It sounds basic, even obvious, but we just *like* people who entertain us. Our defenses lower, and now, we're ready to listen.

CHAPTER 6

INCLUDE 3D OBJECTS

MAKE IT SURPRISING

ANALYZE THEM ON A DEEPER LEVEL

GIVE THE PITCH IN THE RIGHT ORDER

INCLUDE 3D OBJECTS

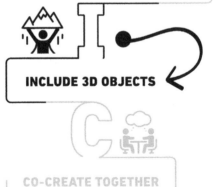

CO-CREATE TOGETHER

We Are *All* Visual Learners

Of all the various myths about education, perhaps the most pervasive is the myth of "different learning styles." Specifically, the theory goes that students' learning styles can be broken down into three types: visual, auditory, and kinesthetic (VAK). Most of us probably grew up accepting this and trying to diagnose what kind of learner we were. The theory took hold in the 1990s, and as recently as 2020, according to a systemic review of available research, *89 percent of teachers across the world still believe in it*.[21] Unfortunately, the theory is absolutely wrong. VAK theory has never been replicated experimentally, and it has been thoroughly disproven.[22]

The reality is, although all of us have different abilities (some may see better than others, or hear better, or write better), all of us learn and remember best visually. That's because the largest amount of our brain's real estate is dedicated to visual processing—over 50 percent of the cortex, the brain's surface. That's more than all of the other senses combined![23]

But what, then, about people who prefer to listen to audiobooks because their eyes glaze over when they read? There are many reasons people may like to listen to certain content, but we're talking about making memorable pitches, and the evidence is clear—the eyes are the easiest pathway to long-term memory. **Our brains remember pictures much better than they remember words.**[24] It's called the picture superiority effect.

And it's not just about memory. A joint study from the University of Minnesota and 3M demonstrated that "presentations using visual aids were found to be 43 percent more persuasive to get people to take action."[25]

The reason pictures trigger action is that visual memory shares the same part of the brain as what we use to process our emotions, the medial temporal lobe. And emotion, as we've shown, is the key to spurring action. Want to see the difference between two kinds of input and how they make you feel? Look at the below signs and really focus on your body's reaction to both the amount of time it takes to process the information and whether it triggers a need to move your body to avoid the danger.

If you want your pitch to spur the prospect to take action, it must contain visual elements—and we don't just mean PowerPoint images. Level up your presentation with three-dimensional objects—items that make the moment *real*.

Clay Alexander's Bag of Tricks

"People like to touch and feel the Ember mug," says Clay Alexander. That's why every time he walks into a pitch— something he's done hundreds of times—he always starts with what he calls his bag of tricks. "I'm not even sure I would say my *name* before I'd take the mug out of the bag." Clay would unzip a suitcase—for years he used a large leather satchel until it burst through its seams—and takes out a variety of Ember products: prototype plate, the mug, the baby bottle. He hands them out, lets the clients feel their weight and texture. Then he takes out one last item: his patent. That, says Clay, is where people get *really* excited.

Quick question: Have *you* ever seen an actual patent? Held one? If you said no, welcome to the club. Clay says that 99 percent of the humans he's pitched to over the years have never actually seen a physical patent in person before. Patents turn out to be beautiful documents: they come with a gold embossed seal and ribbon and beautifully printed borders, and sometimes they're massive, hundred-page tomes. Even the coolest investors who have held all kinds of shiny technology long before consumers ever saw it, tend to "lose it" when they hold a patent for the first time. And then you get to tell the story, and according to Clay, "you're off and running in the conversation with none of the awkwardness."

It's not just an icebreaker. Research shows that real-world three-dimensional props are significantly more memorable than two-dimensional images or text.[26] The more you can bring your presentation off the screen and into the tactile, physical world, the more likely it is to last in your prospect's mind and make an emotional connection. Moreover, we know that **the longer we touch or hold something, the more we feel ownership over it and the more we want it.**[27] And the more we feel like we already own something, the higher value we place on it.[28]

Admittedly, it's easy for an inventor like Clay to deploy props in his pitch; after all, he's selling a physical object, one meant to be held and used. The same is also true of the people pitching on *Shark Tank*, who always bring their products for the sharks to sample, hold, or even climb inside. *Shark Tank* pitches are designed for television, which means they tend naturally to be visually oriented experiences. But what if the thing you're selling is too big to fit in a suitcase or exists only in code or the cloud? Doesn't matter. Put *something* in their hands. 72andSunny created that elegant magazine for United to read and take home. Diana's friend Sarah created a website to communicate her enthusiasm for an idea. And Joan Wells brings a thoughtful gift to virtually every meeting.

Once you understand the emotional power of sight and touch, you'll never enter a room without a visual element.

Case Study: How the Founders of Square Prioritized Surprise Over Functionality for Their Fundraising Pitch

If you're feeling really bold, don't give them something—*take* something. That's what Jim McKelvey, the founder of Square, did when he started every pitch.[29] He would whip out a piece of hardware—a tiny little white square credit card reader. He'd plug it into his iPhone. Then he'd ask one of the VCs in the room for their credit card, and then *he took their money*. It would be anywhere between \$1 and \$40 (depending on how much he liked the VC in question), but he took it. And he didn't give it back.

Now he had their attention. And that's what he wanted the most. The core of McKelvey's communication strategy is focusing on what he calls moments of attention. He argues that most people overestimate how important their ideas are to whoever's listening. "If you don't begin every breath with this acknowledgment that the person you're speaking to has a bunch of other alternatives, you're going to squander those few seconds of attention." McKelvey assumes that in an hourlong pitch, he may have investors who are only really listening for a minute or two. He is acutely aware of how easily presentations can get tedious. That's why you don't just want to make your presentation interesting; you want to make it *surprising*.

McKelvey actually made sure that the original Square reader didn't work as well as it could have in order to create that element of surprise. Part of the problem with pitching a digital payment method is that however transformative its potential, there's just nothing inherently sexy about swiping a credit card. McKelvey had to find some way of focusing investors' attention on the reader itself—**which is why the original reader was deliberately made too small to read a credit card perfectly.** When you run a card through the Square dongle, the card has to wobble awkwardly. McKelvey first built a different reader, a wider one, that worked smoothly, but he found that the smaller, clunkier one captured people's attention better.

The point, he says, is that "people don't realize how fleeting and precious a moment of true attention is." He sacrificed usability of the hardware itself in exchange for people saying, *What the hell just happened? Show me that again.*

Take It to the Next Level: Create an Immersive Experience

Even if sight is the most direct path to emotional connection, don't stop there. The more senses you can involve in your pitch, the more memorable it will be. That's one reason Clay's bag of tricks works so well.[30] It allows clients to bring multiple senses to bear on the object, which is the fastest way to turn your pitch into an *experience*.

There's a hierarchy of ways to plant memories in a client's brain.[31] It goes like this:

TEXT ONLY < IMAGE ONLY < IMAGE + VIDEO < SOMETHING TANGIBLE < ENGAGE THE FIVE SENSES

Importantly, once you introduce one or two elements that are surprising into your pitch, you also begin to build anticipation. This is a compounding effect of surprising someone. When the brain starts anticipating another exciting moment, it gets locked in.

As a keynote speaker, Diana has learned that you'll never have the audience's attention more than you will in **the first thirty seconds of the speech—she calls it the golden window**—and that if you don't do something interesting or unexpected to build anticipation in that window, you'll start to see a lot of phones come out of people's pockets. But she's also learned that she can't assume that a big opening is enough to *hold* their attention for the full hour of a keynote, and it's certainly not enough to spur them into action.

If you're pitching a room of five strangers, creating an experience is how you drive action. It's no different in a room with a thousand strangers. Diana's goal with each keynote is to get people to make more room in their work for curiosity and innovation, but she knows that she's fighting a lot of natural instincts. If she just *tells* people that it's important to ask better questions or look for their blind spots, they'll nod and shrug and out come the phones.

Instead, she must create an immersive experience in which they make these realizations for themselves. For instance, when Diana is trying to explain how we all have blind spots in our work and our customer relationships, she'll ask everyone in the room, "Raise your hand if you think you're pretty good at breathing."

There are some chuckles, some half-raised hands, lots of looking around the room. It's a silly question.

"Okay, let's do a little experiment," she says playfully. "Stand up." There is a great scraping of chairs. "You're going to put one hand on your chest and one hand on your stomach. And we're all going to take a breath together on the count of three. When you do take the breath, please pay attention to which hand moves more than the other—the one on your chest or the one on your stomach."

At this point, no one is on their phone.

"One…two…three," she counts as the room becomes completely void of any noise. You can hear a pin drop. And when everyone takes a breath in unison, the sound is extraordinary. Imagine—a thousand people suddenly breathe as one. When they sit down again, the energy in the room has changed. They don't know where this is going, but they are *in*.

"Okay! How many of you felt the hand on your chest move?" Two-thirds of the room usually raise their hand. The remaining third felt it in their stomachs.

Diana then explains that the way we breathe isn't a preference, like Coke or Pepsi. There's a scientifically right way to breathe and a wrong way to breathe, and it affects virtually everything in your life: your blood pressure, your digestion, your sleep, even your mood. Studies have shown that when researchers taught people to breathe correctly for twelve weeks, the subjects experienced the same positive benefits as a control group that took antidepressants.

"The way you breathe matters," she says, "and unfortunately, two-thirds of this room is doing it the wrong way." And now, *now* she gets to the point. "Everyone in this room walked in thinking they had breathing figured out." She chuckles. "And that's simply because you've never heard any evidence to the contrary. That's how we are at work: we assume that no news is good news. And yet there are so many parts of what we do every day that aren't working as well as we assume."

Diana can now start to see the audience reflect: *Which parts of my work might have blind spots?* And for the rest of the speech, Diana keeps presenting information this way, building anticipation and then leading them to make the conclusions for themselves in a way that will get them to not only remember the lessons but also act on them.

The power of Diana's presentation doesn't come from the breathing lesson but from the fact that she presents her insights in such unexpected ways that the audience never knows what's coming next—and they can't wait to find out. It is this anticipation of a payoff that leads to a dopamine release in their brains.[32]

When a prospect isn't just listening to a pitch but is actively leaning forward, anticipating what you're going to do next, then you truly have them on your side. That's why you want to make your pitch as *immersive* an experience as possible.

Case Study: How a Construction Company Landed a $500 Million Project in Ten Minutes

No one expects a construction company to have a sense of humor.

In 2005, Paul Neidlein was the business development manager at Turner construction, when a large international developer announced it was coming to Kansas City to build a huge new water park. A $500 million project, it instantly became *the* prize for every general contractor in town. It would have been a transformational project for any firm but especially for Turner, which was by no means the biggest in the city. So right from the jump, Paul and Turner decided to Go Big or Go Home.

What followed was a multiyear effort of getting to know the water park developer and their vision. The company was based in a town called New Braunfels, Texas, near San Antonio. It was a family business, built up over decades.

The family invited Paul and his boss to try out one of their water parks before it opened for the day. So they showed up an hour early, in swimsuits and suntan lotion. They had a blast and came away understanding that *fun* was at the heart of the company they were pitching.

Paul knew that his firm wasn't going to win on price or experience, so he decided to create a fun magic moment.

Paul turned the 18,000 square feet of Turner corporate office space on the twelfth floor of a generic office building into a water park. He and his team decorated every square foot of the office in the same style as the water park they had visited. They filled the space with 250 inflatable inner tubes, dozens of beach balls, and as Paul described, every other imaginable beach toy.

One thing Paul had noticed the morning that he got to explore the park early was that all of the water park employees wore neon T-shirts color-coded to their jobs. So Paul re-created the effect with every Turner employee—neon shirts with their department on the back.

The moment the clients walked out of the elevator, Paul could see the delight on their faces. They felt right at home. "We think it really showed them that we'd been paying attention the whole time. That it wasn't a transactional sales pitch. It made them see that we understood what made them appealing to their customers."

The Turner employees didn't just continue working at their desks; they greeted the water park executives by kicking beach balls at them and waving hello, just like employees of the water park would do.

The whole walk-through of the office took just ten minutes. Then they went into the conference room for the formal presentation, which was scheduled for three hours. Halfway through the presentation, says Paul, "they interrupted us and said, 'You can stop. We're going to hire you. You understand what we're trying to do better than we ever could have imagined.'" They not only cut the presentation short; they admitted they were supposed to meet with one of the other finalists the next day. They didn't even need to hear what that firm had to say. Instead, they asked if they could have some of the T-shirts that Paul had made to take with them to show their team back home.

That is the power of a magic moment: years of relationship building and listening, and in the end, ten minutes made the difference. Those ten minutes were all it took to forge a lasting emotional connection and push the clients irrevocably toward a decision worth half a billion dollars.

Importantly, though, Paul says that the reason they were willing to try something as bonkers as turning their office into a water park was because they knew they *weren't* the favorite to win. If they'd felt more secure about being the biggest or the best firm in the mix, or if they'd felt it was their job to lose, they'd have been more likely to play it safe. But even so, the whole time, he was deeply nervous the whole shtick would fail. He remembers thinking, "Will they get it? Will they even care about this stuff? Or will they just care about how much it costs?" In the end, Paul was willing to try it *because* Turner was a long shot to win. "When you have no business winning, you have nothing to lose. That's when you say, 'Let's do something crazy,' and a lot of the time, crazy wins."

CHAPTER 7

CO-CREATE TOGETHER

MAKE IT SURPRISING

ANALYZE THEM ON A DEEPER LEVEL

GIVE THE PITCH IN THE RIGHT ORDER

INCLUDE 3D OBJECTS

CO-CREATE TOGETHER

> "People believe that if they have a good idea, it will sell itself. It won't."

That's from Kimberly D. Elsbach, associate professor in the Graduate School of Management at the University of California at Davis.[33] Elsbach spent six years shadowing Hollywood executives as they entertained dozens of pitches from screenwriters. Her goal was to uncover which pitches got the most traction. She writes:

> All too often, entrepreneurs, sales executives, and marketing managers go to great lengths to show how their new business plans or creative concepts are practical and high margin—only to be rejected by corporate decision makers who don't seem to understand the real value of the ideas. Why does this happen?[34]

The problem, she found, was that the clients hearing the pitch aren't just judging the idea; they're judging the people pitching it, and very quickly, they slot those people into stereotypes. "So the first thing to realize," she writes in the *Harvard Business Review*, "when you're preparing to make a pitch to strangers is that your audience is going to put you into a box. And they're going to do it really fast." The reason they do this is that **when evaluating a flurry of new ideas, as most high-level decision makers do, few people have the bandwidth to assess each one on its objective merits.** Instead, they're using stereotypes to put the person pitching through a process of elimination—one that is brutally hard to survive. This instinct "is so firmly hardwired into human psychology that only conscious discipline can counteract it." This is why we have been so insistent throughout this book about the importance of establishing a connection before the actual pitch meeting.

Elsbach says that the best way to get yourself out of that box is to turn the person you are pitching into a co-creator. While she saw this in only 25 percent of the pitches she observed, individuals who found opportunities for the client they were pitching to shine and share their creativity as a collaborator had the best chance of closing the deal.

> **"The invitation to collaborate
> on an idea is a seduction."
> —OLIVER STONE**

In a B2B setting, the process is similar. Clay Alexander says, "If I walked into a room and said, 'I'm Clay Alexander. I'm an inventor. Look at this fully baked thing. I have all the answers,' I'd never land a single deal." He goes in with his concept, then solicits the client's input. He doesn't even see the pitch as trying to make a sale but rather to cement a *partnership*. For instance, when selling the cold box to Cardinal Health, he had specific moments in the presentation that were pauses for collaboration. He asked the clients to tell him which sizes and capacities for boxes would best work with their shipping methods, and he let them take control of that part of the meeting. By the end, Clay has a better understanding of the client, and they have a greater sense of ownership over the finished product.

Case Study: How Vince Kadlubek Got George R. R. Martin to Invest in Meow Wolf

Through the doors of a once-crumbling bowling alley in Santa Fe is a psychedelic pocket universe unlike anything else in our reality. Phosphorescent forests, hallucinogenic robots, corridors of shimmering neon, a fridge that teleports you to an alternate dimension...this is Meow Wolf, a production company that creates immersive multimedia experiences and has raised over $170 million in investment to expand its concept. And the most astonishing thing about the organization might be that it exists at all.

Meow Wolf began as a collective of Santa Fe artists who felt utterly disenchanted with the traditional gallery-based art world. Co-creation, in a very real sense, was at the heart of everything they did. They harvested materials from dumpsters, lived together in a house, and dedicated everything they had to their vision. Eventually, stretched to the breaking point financially and emotionally, they knew that if they were to have any chance of making their creation sustainable, they needed two things: a building and money. Lots of money.

Their first installation was to be called the House of Eternal Return. Vince Kadlubek, one of the co-founders, found a derelict bowling alley in Santa Fe to be the flagship location. It would cost nearly $3 million to purchase and renovate, and at that point, the artists involved in Meow Wolf were broke. "Like broke, broke, broke. We did not have any money. We all worked in food delivery, or restaurant work, or hotels."[35] In a Hail Mary effort, Kadlubek reached out to Santa Fe's most famous citizen, George R. R. Martin, fantasy novelist and screenwriter, best known as the creator of the show *Game of Thrones*, to see if he could help.

Kadlubek and Martin had met before, but it was a small connection at best. Kadlubek's first pitch was the cold email seeking to get the meeting. He used all the psychographic research about Martin that he had to put together an emotional appeal. "I knew he was interested in preserving elements of Santa Fe. I shared my big crazy idea and suggested that he could be our champion. All I needed was a meeting."

When Martin agreed to take the meeting, Kadlubek decided that the best way to turn him into a co-creator was to meet him at the bowling alley itself. "The bowling alley was the environment of possibility. During the walk-through, there were some moments where I was consciously giving him space to be the one to come up with ideas. I would watch to see what he was interested in and then dive deeper into the possibilities. I wanted to create space for him to play with us."

To hear Martin talk about it, it was as if Kadlubek was reading his inner thoughts: "The Victorian house lost in time and space, other dimensions, other times, a secret story you would have to decipher...he was pushing all my buttons there," Martin remembers. "He probably knew they were my buttons."[36]

Martin was enchanted by the possibilities that they dreamed up together that day. He agreed to buy the building for Meow Wolf, and as Kadlubek calls it, became the first domino. Martin's investment allowed them to raise $3 million for that first permanent exhibit, which swiftly became a sensation in the art world. Eight years later, they're on track to open new locations in Denver and Las Vegas.

Case Study: How the US Naval Academy Uses Co-creation to Recruit Student Athletes

A few years ago, the Naval Academy in Annapolis, Maryland hired DI to design the interactive displays in their brand-new recruitment center. The Naval Academy had a problem: it's difficult to recruit the best athletes in the country—especially in marquee sports like football and basketball—when part of the deal is that those athletes can't play professionally after graduation but instead have to do at least four years of military service.

DI's job was to create an experience that would show the athletes who visited just what it would mean to them—and their families—to play for Navy and, therefore, to join the Navy. The old recruitment center was a very traditional, 1960s-era design. There was a hall of ship models and photos of illustrious alumni, like Senator John McCain. It was precisely what one would expect when visiting an iconic institution like the Naval Academy—and that was the problem. People who had graduated from the Academy might feel an emotional connection to such a place, but recruits wouldn't. It was, in other words, an entirely satisfactory experience.

DI created new displays throughout the recruitment center so that they could be customized based on the visitor. So, for instance, if the women's soccer team invites recruits for a tour, all of the interactive technology will highlight soccer images because conventional static imagery that emphasizes bigger sports like football will do little to impress a women's soccer recruit.

The main co-creative element is an interactive display called Who Will You Become? which allows visitors to project an image of themselves on a screen wearing different uniforms, whether athletic or Naval, and even send those photographs to people back home. At that moment, visitors receive one of the most powerful messages you can convey to a potential recruit or client: *You're one of us. You belong here.*

The last stop on the tour is a room with a 180-degree immersive theater—the screen wraps around the walls and goes from floor to ceiling. And when the screen switches on, suddenly the recruits are thundering out of the tunnel with the rest of the team and onto the field. It's the Army–Navy game, the military Super Bowl. The crowd roars. Fireworks burst. The Blue Angels streak overhead. The whole thing is larger than life. You can feel the bass throughout your body. It's this freeing, jubilant moment you feel down to your core.

A lot of institutions, especially storied, prestigious ones, often forget about the real reason why students wind up choosing a school: they're looking for that *Field of Dreams* moment, where they find themselves drawn to a place, even though they can't say exactly why. They just know it feels right. DI's goal at the Naval Academy was to create a space that gave the school the best chance of generating that gut feeling, by transforming a simple college visit into a deeply emotional experience.

When You Co-create the Pitch, You Cease to Be Adversaries and You Start Playing for the Same Team

Jim McKelvey, the founder of Square, had a very clever slide in his pitch deck designed to elicit co-creation. It was titled "140 Reasons Why This Idea Will Fail." And every time he brought up the slide, it would change the tenor of the meeting.[37] "If you think about most VC pitches," he says, "they're these terrible attack-and-defend spectacles, where the entrepreneurs are on the attack, basically lying, trying to get these investors' money, and the investors are defending, trying not to be taken in by the lies. They're trying to punch holes in the entrepreneurs' pitches. It's very adversarial." But McKelvey and his partner, Twitter founder Jack Dorsey, didn't want any part of that "standard process." So they decided to be utterly candid about every problem they could foresee (they chose the number 140 because Dorsey had an emotional connection to that number). It took Jim and Jack an entire week to come up with all 140 of them. In the end, some were real, like "attacked by Amazon" or "malware," others were a little more out there ("Jack kills Jim," "robot uprising").

"And then, in the pitch, as we'd discuss these problems, the venture capitalist would tell us how they could help us." In fact, one VC came right out and said, "I'm on the board of Amazon. If you take our money, I can stop Amazon from targeting you"—which is ultimately what happened: They took the investor's money, and he made important arguments within Amazon on their behalf. But the crucial point here is how the emotional energy in the room shifted. The VCs weren't trying to poke holes in McKelvey's pitch anymore; they were trying to *fill* them.

Co-creation helps us shift suspicion into a problem-solving partnership.

CHAPTER 8

EVERY PITCH NEEDS A MAGIC STRATEGY

It's hard for humans to generate feelings toward statistics.

Below are two pitches. As you read them, ask yourself which one is more likely to get you to make a donation.

A) Any money that you donate will go to Rokia, a seven-year-old girl who lives in Mali in Africa. Rokia is desperately poor and faces a threat of severe hunger, even starvation. Her life will be changed for the better as a result of your financial gift. With your support and the support of other caring sponsors, Save the Children will work with Rokia's family and other members of the community to help feed and educate her and provide her with basic medical care.

B) Food shortages in Malawi are affecting more than 3 million children. In Zambia, severe rainfall deficits have resulted in a 42 percent drop in maize production from 2000. As a result, an estimated 3 million Zambians face hunger. Four million Angolans—one-third of the population—have been forced to flee their homes. More than 11 million people in Ethiopia need immediate food assistance.

If you picked A, you're in the majority, according to a study from a team of Wharton marketing professors (who created these two hypothetical pitches as part of their study).[38] Specifically, the researchers wanted to understand why, when raising money for charity, appealing to a donor's heart is orders of magnitude more effective than appealing to their head. Despite the power of statistics to demonstrate the scope of devastation, individual stories are far more likely to drive donations.

The reason, according to this study, is that Rokia is someone we can identify with. We can feel for her in a way that we cannot *feel* statistics, no matter how devastating. In fact, statistics only get *more* impersonal the bigger and scarier they get. According to the Wharton study, "the more statistical information a group was given about the general plight of a certain people, the less generous they became."

The most critical aspect of a Go Big or Go Home pitch is that it must trigger an emotional response in order to lodge itself in the prospect's long-term memory, like piece of corn stuck in their teeth, impossible to get out, so they keep toying with it all day. What we know doesn't work is relying merely on logic and statistics.

Instead, we must plan out our pitches to engineer those moments of magic and decide when they will take place. And while each of the five tools we've described will help you stand out, their value compounds when you combine them together. We call it "stacking."

Case Study: How DI Won the Las Vegas Raiders Torch Project

From the beginning, DI knew there were two challenges with this pitch: first, they wouldn't have the opportunity to pitch the final decision maker, owner Mark Davis, personally, and second, there was already a favorite going in. And it wasn't DI.

In 2018, the Las Vegas Raiders were constructing their new stadium, and its centerpiece was to be a colossal nine-story torch in honor of their legendary owner, the late Al Davis. The torch would be visible from every seat in the stadium as well from the nearby Vegas strip. That was the idea anyway. DI was invited to submit a bid to build the thing.

In initial conversations, DI learned that they were part of a small group of companies that had been selected because they were capable of such a project. There was a fixed budget, a tight timeline (NFL opening day doesn't wait), and very challenging design constraints that had been set by both the architect and Raiders' ownership: specifically, the Raiders wanted the entire surface of the torch to be smooth and unbroken, like the iconic mirrored Bean in Chicago's Millennium Park—except five times the size. At first, DI went to another company and asked if they wanted to partner up to create the torch, and the company politely declined. They said it was impossible, given the budget.

But DI went to work, deploying a Wing Team that combined technologists, their best engineers and fabricators, and the Innovation Lab, eventually coming up with a design solution that they thought worked. It was an elegant approach and within the budget and time frame. When DI presented this solution to the architects and a group of execs from the Raiders, they liked it…but not enough. Even though they passed DI onto the next round, it was clear this solution wasn't going to win them the job.

The next month, the client changed the assignment. This time, they had the same design constraints and schedule, but they told everyone to forget about the budget. "Bring us your best ideas," they said. Now it was time to Go Big or Go Home.

Make it Surprising

DI went back to the drawing board to get that perfect, seamless, organic shape. Then, after dozens of ideas had been ruled out, Ben from the Innovation Lab said, "We've got a crazy-ass idea: let's 3D print it!" It may have been crazy, but everyone immediately knew that that was the right answer—it was innovative, it was bold, and most of all, it was truly the thing DI refers to as NBDB: never been done before. If they could make this work, they knew it would get the Raiders' attention.

The problem was, since it had never been done before, no one knew if they *could* even do it. They had experience 3D printing materials, but nothing at this scale—no one on earth did. On a Friday night, they found out that there was a company in Indiana that made a printer big enough to manage this project. By Sunday, Tucker and an associate were in the car heading there.

It wasn't just a big 3D printer. It was the biggest 3D printer in the world, and it cost $2.2 million. When Tucker met the CEO, he asked if he could talk to someone else who had one of these printers to see if it was up to the job.

"No one has one," said the CEO. He pointed through the window. "You'd be buying the first one."

Within a week, DI's engineers and researchers validated that this was a viable solution. Like the Raiders themselves, it was an approach that was bold and innovative. This wasn't going to be one of a handful of possible solutions DI would pitch; it would be their *only* proposal.

Analyze Them on a Deeper Level

While the Wing Team was proofing the concept, DI also deployed a team that spent several weeks researching the decision makers on the project. In particular, the research team tried to understand what the Raiders franchise cared about and what accomplishments they were most proud of. Through a series of interviews and supporting research, they found that the organization prided itself immensely on its independence and iconoclasm—they always wanted to be the team who bucked tradition, tore up the playbook, and took a bare-knuckle approach to winning. They were never going to be the stuffy, proper, corporate team. They took the name "Raiders" as a mission, not just a brand.

To show how well they understood that mission, DI created a video to launch the pitch. And part of the research was to test the video with their internal advocates inside the Raiders' organization. That was a big move. The internal folks pointed out a person in the video who appeared in a frame or two and said, "Do *not* show that person." DI had barely noticed him, but if the owner saw it, he'd have zeroed in on it and forgotten everything else. Having that insight absolutely saved the pitch.

Give the Pitch in the Right Order

Because the DI team wasn't going to be in the room with the decision makers, that video wound up being the first thing the Raiders' execs saw. But DI didn't fall into the trap of pitching backward because the video didn't tell the story of DI at all. Instead, it told the story of the Raiders. The opening words of the video were, *The Raiders. Las Vegas. Of course. Right out of the Davis playbook. If you're the Raiders, you're not afraid to make the bold move when it's the right thing to do.*

DI's message was clear: If any team was going to make the world's largest 3D printed element, it should be the Raiders.

Include 3D Objects

The video was accompanied by a sample of what the gigantic 3D printer could create. It wasn't a model or a mockup—everyone was using those. What DI sent was something that looked like it came from outer space.

The way the presentations were made was that once the decision makers watched the videos in their conference room, they would go out into an adjacent warehouse that housed all of the mockups of the various elements that would go into the new stadium. And there, amid all the various models, was a ten-foot-tall, 350-pound monolith. It was a single 3D-printed chunk of the torch—one of 225 curving panels that would interlock to build it. DI had driven a truck to the warehouse and dropped it off there, so that as the Raiders executives went through this large warehouse, making all kinds of decisions, suddenly they would see this giant towering element made from a material they had never seen before.

Do you remember the scene at the start of *2001: A Space Odyssey*? The apes awake and out of nowhere, there is an immense black slab before them. They don't know what it is or where it came from, but the apes go berserk, driven mad by the sudden mysterious presence. The Raiders brass didn't start shrieking or pawing at it, but the effect was powerful. Combined with the video, the whole experience engaged as many senses as DI could affect in a remote fashion.

Co-create Together

From the beginning, DI's designers worked as closely as they could with the architect who devised the vision of the torch, collaborating intimately with him on the pitch because they knew he had the ear of Mark Davis, who was involved in nearly every element of that stadium. So throughout the concept, testing, and design process, they invited the architect to visit DI as much as possible to help the team imagine what could be: something that had never existed before and could be customized based on their needs. The architect's suggestions were invaluable.

From start to finish, DI's pitch was intended to connect with the Raiders on an emotional level that said, *You don't believe in taking the traditional approach, and neither do we.* A few days after the remote presentation, Tucker got the call: they loved it. DI had won.

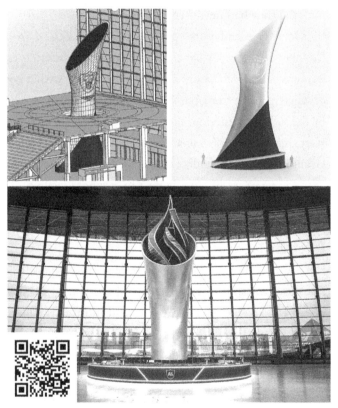

Conceptual Design and Architecture by MANICA Architecture.

EPILOGUE

That's it. That's the book. We've shared everything we've learned about creating the types of presentations that stand out and help you win.

If you've got a presentation that matters, we hope that this book serves as your blueprint for adding some magic to the experience. And although not every Go Big or Go Home pitch will lead to a win, they will almost always start a relationship with the prospect or lead to other opportunities in the future. And most importantly, your Go Big or Go Home pitch will help communicate your personality and how much enthusiasm you have for the work that you do.

One of our early readers pointed out that "it's impossible to add moments of magic to a presentation without really caring about both your audience and the work that you do. If you don't mean it, it'll be obvious."

We couldn't agree more. This methodology is a way to channel your enthusiasm into a presentation that helps them feel it.

At the very least, we hope this book sparks a conversation on your team about what kind of emotional experience your pitches can create and whether there are any opportunities to use one of the tools described in the previous chapters to add some emotional peaks, some connection, and some moments of magic that might help you seal more deals. If it helps, feel free to copy and use the handy worksheet on the next page to plan out your pitches.

For us, Go Big or Go Home has become much more than a business practice. It is a way to inject a lot more fun into our lives. We hope it does the same for you!

MAGIC PITCH PLAN

PITCH	DATE

M — **MAKE IT SURPRISING**

What surprising details could you add to the pitch?
Ex. Gifts, experiences, or stories.

A — **ANALYZE THEM ON A DEEPER LEVEL**

How could you tailor the pitch so that they feel
it was created just for them?

G — **GIVE THE PITCH IN THE RIGHT ORDER**

How will you show them that you
understand their perspective? How will
it be about their story?

I — **INCLUDE 3D OBJECTS**

What 3D objects can you include with the
presentation? Remember, they don't have to be
related to your product/service.

C — **CO-CREATE TOGETHER**

What parts of the presentation will you give
them the opportunity to co-create with you?

**DOWNLOAD THIS WORKSHEET AND OTHER
GO BIG OR GO HOME MATERIALS AT GOBIGBONUS.COM**

NOMINATE A NATURAL

If you loved the book and thought of someone in your life who is already a natural of the Go Big or Go Home method, we want to celebrate them with you by sending them a FREE copy of the book!

We've created an entire website: **www.NominateANatural.com** where you can submit a nomination form, sharing an example of a magic moment they created to close a deal.

Maybe we'll use their story in the next version of this book!

All your questions about the nomination and logistics of the free book will be answered on the site.

We cannot wait to hear about the Go Big or Go Home natural in your life.

HOW MANY STARS WOULD YOU GIVE THIS BOOK?

Reviews are *the* most powerful tools to grow the reach of a book! Our ambitious goal (we're totally putting it out there) is to sell 1 million copies of *Go Big or Go Home*. And honest reviews of the book will help bring it to the attention of other readers.

If you got just one takeaway from this book, we would be so grateful if you would spend one minute leaving a review. It can be as short as you like.

You can get right to the review page by going to **www.GoBigBookReview.com**.

Thank you so much!

ACKNOWLEDGMENTS

We want to start by thanking Tom Collins, who brought us together and thought that there might be an interesting collaboration between us. Boy, was he right.

We want to thank Sam Ashworth, our editor on the project. Sam helped every case study leap off the page and Sam's own stories, like his experience grading SAT essays, helped turn this book into an experience that you just want to share with others.

We want to thank the talented DI staff who served as our inspiration for the Go Big or Go Home method outlined in this book, especially Justin Wood, Drew Berst, and the many talented members of the Innovation Lab who have helped DI turn LTF ideas into reality many, many times. We'd like to thank Melinda Sanchez for helping us bring the visual elements of this book to life and a big thank-you to JC Hendricks and the Creative team for turning this book into a magical experience.

And a special shout-out to Zachary Hamby, a Greek mythology high school teacher who loves to draw. Zachary helped us create the visual representations of so many of the big ideas we wanted to share in the book.

We are so grateful to each and every Go Big practitioner who took the time to share their story, at times divulging some of their secret sauce for your benefit and ours. And we're equally grateful to everyone who agreed to our interviews even if their stories didn't make the final version of the book. Your belief in this idea was very meaningful to us and we heard from many of you that our interviews were a good reminder that we always need to think differently about how we pitch.

Our next thank-you goes out to someone who doesn't even know about this book at the time of publication, but he's responsible for the title. We were introduced to Kid Super by a friend and Go Big or Go Home natural, Sam Demma. Sam shared with us an interview with Kid Super in which he detailed his elaborate pitches and general business philosophy. An hour and twenty minutes into the YouTube video, as Kid Super is explaining how he got into Paris Fashion Week, he shares an article from *Vogue* that says he should be recognized for his go big or go home antics, and he reflects in the video, "That really was the motto, Go Big or Go Home!"

We want to thank all of the amazing individuals who read early versions of the book and provided much needed feedback and guidance.

Finally, we want to thank you for reading this book and helping us spread the message. We don't want this book to be a secret and we'd love your help in telling others about it! Whether you gift your copy to a friend, visit NominateANatural.com to acknowledge someone who already exemplifies the tools in the book, or just take a picture of the book and tag a friend on social media who you think could benefit from it, we would so appreciate these efforts!

And don't forget, you can always text us at 816-399-0084 to discuss how to bring the Go Big or Go Home method to your organization.

APPENDIX

Rather than include a traditional "About the Authors" section, we're attaching psychographic reports on the authors that were compiled by Cameron Sullivan based on publicly available information. We hope these reports can help you understand what kind of research some of your competitors might be doing for the biggest deals.

Tucker Trotter Biography and Key Facts

As a child, Tucker was "relentlessly curious" and an early inventor who made his own toys; he went on to graduate from design school and worked his way up from an internship at Dimensional Innovations to become the CEO.

- Beginning at a very young age, Tucker began sketching and investigating and inventing. Tucker would include written pitches for his inventions explaining how they worked.

- When Tucker was in the second grade, his parents divorced and his mother moved Tucker and his sister to deep southern Missouri, where the family built a three-story teepee. Tucker participated in the construction of the teepee, which he credits with teaching him about construction. Tucker said the isolation and wilderness drove him to draw and invent more frequently.

- Tucker graduated from the University of Kansas in 1997 with a Bachelor of Fine Art, Industrial Design. To graduate, Tucker needed an internship. He had just created and sold a patent and started a business, but this did not count. Tucker took an internship at what is now Dimensional Innovations.

Under Tucker's leadership, Dimensional Innovations has expanded internationally, and Tucker has personally led or worked on over 200 projects around the world. Tucker's cutting-edge works have gained notoriety.

- Tucker's notable work includes the giant library books gracing the Kansas City Library downtown parking garage, the HyVee Hot Zone at Arrowhead Stadium, and the University of Kansas's Allen Fieldhouse.

- Tucker's portfolio encompasses the NFL, MLB, NHL, NBA, NCAA, and collegiate sports, along with major installations in museums, hall of fames, and entertainment districts across the country.

- Tucker and Dimensional Innovations designed, created, and installed the world's largest 3D-printed object, the Al Davis Memorial Torch at Allegiant Stadium in Las Vegas.

  - It took eighteen Dimensional Innovations employees 50,000 hours over a year to construct the torch.

  - Dimensional Innovations was the first company to use the Large-Scale Additive Manufacturing 3D printer to build a finished architectural structure. The printer had not been developed for producing structures.

Tucker has worked hard to create a culture of trust and respect at Dimensional Innovations.

- Tucker has made a commitment to upholding the values Dimensional Innovations stands for, including process, collaboration, diversity and inclusion, communication, empowerment, transparency, and vulnerability.

Tucker is passionate about giving back to his community and has participated in many community-building projects.

- Tucker credits his grandfather Fredrick McCoy with inspiring his passion to give back to his community. McCoy was a plastic surgeon who donated a lot of his time to children's hospitals working on cleft palates.

- Tucker serves as the trustee of the Fredrick J. McCoy Endowment Fund for the Cleft and Craniofacial Clinic at Children's Mercy Hospital in Kansas City.

- Dimensional Innovations worked to make the '50s-themed diner and theater at Children's Mercy Hospital more accessible for children in wheelchairs. Tucker claims the features of the theater get kids moving and distracts them from their pain, which speeds up healing and requires less narcotics in treatment.

- Tucker was a founding partner of the Parade of Hearts, a coalition of more than a dozen Kansas City businesses helping to raise funds for sectors most impacted by the pandemic through decorative heart structures throughout the region.

- Dimensional Innovations designed a face shield early in the COVID-19 pandemic and released the plans for free.

- Tucker established the Dimensional Innovations Foundation, an employee-funded 501(c)(3) nonprofit.

Tucker lives a very active lifestyle, enjoys many outdoor activities including hunting and fishing, mountain climbing, and lacrosse.

- Tucker has held hunting and fishing licenses in Alaska and Missouri.

- Tucker is photographed mountain climbing on his social media pages.

Sources used:

- OP Chamber Executive Leadership Series—Tucker Trotter video
- LexisNexis search
- Children's Mercy, Cleft Palate Program website
- *Kansas City Business Journal* article
- Tucker Trotter Facebook
- Tucker Trotter Twitter

Full name: Tucker David Trotter

DOB: June 6, 1972

Family: Wife, Mandi Trotter; three children, one boy and two girls

Twitter: @TuckerTrotter

LinkedIn: www.linkedin.com/in/tuckertrotter/

Website: www.dimin.com

Education: 1992–1997: Bachelor of Fine Art, Industrial Design, University of Kansas

Diana Kander Biography and Key Facts

Diana has lived the American dream as a refugee from the Soviet Union as a child; she went on to graduate Georgetown Law and become a bestselling author, successful entrepreneur, and keynote speaker.

- Diana was born in the former Soviet Union in Odessa, Ukraine. She immigrated to America in 1989 at the age of seven as her family fled religious persecution. She and her parents spoke no English when they arrived. Diana became a naturalized

American citizen and was an entrepreneur even in middle school as she found bargains at flea markets that she sold to her classmates at a markup.

- Diana's parents worked jobs at TJMaxx and Pizza Hut just to make ends meet. They went on to start a company, a dental laboratory, out of their basement, which grew into a successful business that is still around today.

- Diana majored in political science at the University of Missouri–Kansas City before attending Georgetown Law.

- After law school, Diana worked briefly as an attorney at a major law firm before becoming an entrepreneur. She participated in multiple startups where she turned a "few thousand dollars of capital into millions."

- In 2014, Diana wrote her first book, *All In Startup*, which became a *New York Times* Bestseller. This helped further launch her career as a keynote speaker and innovation consultant.

- Today, Diana works as a keynote speaker, innovation consultant, podcast host, author, and more. She's helped major companies like Siemens, Teva

Pharmaceuticals, Ford, H&R Block, YPO, and more through innovation consulting and speeches. On one project, she helped a team generate an extra $8 million in revenue in her first week.

Diana's husband is former Missouri Secretary of State Jason Kander.

- Diana married her high school sweetheart, Jason Kander, and they have two children, True and Bella. They first met in high school as they were debate team opponents at rival schools.

- Jason is the former Missouri Secretary of State and an army veteran who served in Afghanistan. He narrowly lost a bid for Senate in Missouri in 2016. After, he explored a presidential bid and then ran for Mayor of Kansas City before dropping out of the race to receive treatment for his PTSD from his military service. Diana and Jason have bravely spoken publicly about their struggles with PTSD, the effect it has had on their family, and the benefits of treatment.

- Jason now works as President of National Expansion at Veterans Community Project, a nonprofit that provides housing and services for homeless veterans.

- Jason is the author of two *New York Times* Bestsellers: *Invisible Storm* (2022) detailing his PTSD diagnosis and recovery and *Outside the Wire* (2018) outlining his lessons learned in politics and military service.

Diana's family motto is "tikkun olam," which is Hebrew for "repair the world," which is "behind everything they do."

- Diana has said her family's motto is "tikkun olam," which is Hebrew for "repair the world." She has said it drives everything they do, which is evident from their public service, community outreach, and nonprofit work.

- Diana has served on the Goodwill Board of Directors for both the St. Louis and Kansas City regions. She has also served as a general board member for the Jewish Community Relations Bureau/American Jewish Committee in Kansas City.

Sources used:

- Diana Kander Twitter
- StartUpGrind article
- KeySpeakers website
- Eventbrite event description
- *Columbia Missourian* article
- Startland News article

- KCUR article
- Diana Kander LinkedIn
- St. Louis Public Radio article
- *Independent Banker* article
- LexisNexis search
- DianaKander.com

ENDNOTES

1   Manda Mahoney, "The Subconscious Mind of the Consumer (and How to Reach It)," Harvard Business School Working Knowledge, January 13, 2003, https://hbswk.hbs.edu/item/the-subconscious-mind-of-the-consumer-and-how-to-reach-it.

2   Samuel M. McClure et al., "Neural Correlates of Behavioral Preference for Culturally Familiar Drinks," Neuron 44, no. 2 (2004): 379–87, https://doi.org/10.1016/j.neuron.2004.09.019.

3   Federation of American Societies for Experimental Biology (FASEB), "Don't Like the Food? Try Paying More," Newswise, April 29, 2014, https://www.newswise.com/articles/don-t-like-the-food-try-paying-more?sc=sphr&xy=10003935.

4   William H. Shrank et al., "Patients' Perceptions of Generic Medications," Health Affairs 28, no. 2 (March–April 2009): 546–56, https://doi.org/10.1377%2Fhlthaff.28.2.546.

5   M. Price, "Placebos Produce Effect Even When Patients Know It's Just Sugar," Monitor on Psychology 42, no. 3 (March 2011): 10, https://www.apa.org/monitor/2011/03/placebos.

6   Roger Koenig-Robert and Joel Pearson, "Decoding the Contents and Strength of Imagery before Volitional Engagement," Scientific Reports 9, no. 3504 (March 5, 2019), https://doi.org/10.1038/s41598-019-39813-y.

7   Sam Nathan and Karl Schmidt, "From Promotion to Emotion: Connecting B2B Customers to Brands," Think with Google, October 2013, https://www.thinkwithgoogle.com/consumer-insights/consumer-trends/promotion-emotion-b2b/; CEB Marketing Leadership Council and Google, "From Promotion to Emotion: Connecting B2B Customers to Brands" (white paper, 2013), https://plan2brand.com/wp-content/uploads/2015/07/CEB_Promotion_to_Emotion_whitepaper.pdf.

8   Sam Ashworth, interview with authors.

9   Literally since 1885, when German psychologist
    Hermann Ebbinghaus published his "Forgetting Curve"
    study. In 2015, a team sought to replicate his study and
    found that both his methodology and conclusions held
    up 130 years later.

10 Praveen Shrestha, "Ebbinghaus Forgetting Curve,"
    Psychestudy, November 17, 2017, https://www
    .psychestudy.com/cognitive/memory/ebbinghaus
    -forgetting-curve.

11 Daniel Kahneman, "Two Selves," in Thinking, Fast and
    Slow (New York: Farrar, Straus & Giroux, 2011), 377–85.
    The book explains the peak-end rule, a cognitive bias that
    impacts how people remember past events. The peak-end
    rule states that individuals do not remember or base their
    opinion of an experience based on the full experience, but
    instead, they over-index the most emotionally intense
    part (whether good or bad) and the end. The peak-
    end rule is grounded in research conducted by Daniel
    Kahneman and Barbara Fredrickson in 1993. (See also
    Columbia University Irving Medical Center, "Why Are
    Memories Attached to Emotions So Strong?" July 13,
    2020, https://www.cuimc.columbia.edu/news/why-are-
    memories-attached-emotions-so-strong; The University of
    Queensland Australia, "What Makes Memories Stronger?"
    accessed August 29, 2022, https://qbi.uq.edu.au/
    brain-basics/memory/what-makes-memories-stronger.)

12 Emily Kwong, "Understanding Unconscious Bias," July 15, 2020, in Short Wave, produced by NPR, podcast, 14:16, https://www.npr.org/transcripts/891140598.

13 Louise Story, "Anywhere the Eye Can See, It's Likely to See an Ad," New York Times, January 15, 2007, https://web.archive.org/web/20200320191358/https:/www.nytimes.com/2007/01/15/business/media/15everywhere.html; Nadia, "How Many Ads Do We See a Day?" Siteefy (blog), last modified May 13, 2022, https://siteefy.com/how-many-ads-do-we-see-a-day/.

14 Before she agreed to the acquisition, Wells made sure that Augeo held the same beliefs about investing first. So the practice continues!

15 CEB Marketing Leadership Council and Google, "From Promotion to Emotion."

16 Nathan and Schmidt, "From Promotion to Emotion"; CEB Marketing Leadership Council and Google, "From Promotion to Emotion."

17 Chris Voss, "How I Build TRUST in Negotiations," The Black Swan Group, July 5, 2018, YouTube video, 1:02:16, https://www.youtube.com/watch?v=jLQiemA7a_k.

18 Adrian F. Ward, "The Neuroscience of Everybody's Favorite Topic," Scientific American, July 16, 2013, https://www.scientificamerican.com/article/the-neuroscience-of-everybody-favorite-topic-themselves/.

19 Inc. Staff, "Watch Mark Cuban's Best-Ever Sales Pitch," Inc., May 15, 2017, https://www.inc.com/video/watch-mark-cubans-best-ever-sales-pitch.html.

20 Callie Caplan, "Mavericks Secure Longest Sellout Streak in NBA History," The Dallas Morning News, February 12, 2020, https://www.dallasnews.com/sports/mavericks/2020/02/13/mavericks-secure-longest-sellout-streak-in-nba-history/.

21 Philip M. Newton and Atharva Salvi, "How Common Is Belief in the Learning Styles Neuromyth, and Does It Matter? A Pragmatic Systematic Review," Frontiers in Education 5, no. 602451 (December 2020), https://doi.org/10.3389/feduc.2020.602451.

22 Olga Khazan, "The Myth of 'Learning Styles,'" The Atlantic, April 11, 2018, https://www.theatlantic.com/science/archive/2018/04/the-myth-of-learning-styles/557687/.

23 Susan Hagen, "The Mind's Eye," Rochester Review 74, no. 4 (March–April 2012): 32–37, https://www.rochester.edu/pr/Review/V74N4/0402_brainscience.html.

24 Margaret Anne Defeyter, Riccardo Russo, and Pamela Louise McPartlin, "The Picture Superiority Effect in Recognition Memory: A Developmental Study Using the Response Signal Procedure," Cognitive Development 24, no. 3 (July–September 2009): 265–73, https://doi.org/10.1016/j.cogdev.2009.05.002; Peter S. Houts et al., "The Role of Pictures in Improving Health Communication: A Review of Research on Attention, Comprehension, Recall, and Adherence," Patient Education and Counseling 61, no. 2 (May 2006): 173–90, https://doi.org/10.1016/j.pec.2005.05.004.

25 Douglas R. Vogel, Gary W. Dickson, and John A. Lehman, "Persuasion and the Role of Visual Presentation Support: The UM/3M Study," Working Paper Series, no. MISRC-WP-86-11 (June 1986), http://thinktwicelegal.com/olio/articles/persuasion_article.pdf. The study also revealed that people's perceptions of a presenter can vary dramatically depending on whether or not she uses visuals. People who watched the presentation with accompanying visuals rated the presenter—who was consistent

across all groups—as more concise, professional, clear, persuasive, and interesting than those who saw the presentation without visuals.

26 Jacqueline C. Snow et al., "Real-World Objects Are More Memorable than Photographs of Objects," Frontiers in Human Neuroscience 8, no. 837 (October 2014), https://doi.org/10.3389/fnhum.2014.00837.

27 Andrea Thompson, "Study: You Touch It, You Buy It," Live Science, January 16, 2009, https://www.livescience.com/3241-study-touch-buy.html.

28 Daniel Kahneman, Jack L. Knetsch, and Richard H. Thaler, "Experimental Tests of the Endowment Effect and the Coase Theorem," Journal of Political Economy 98, no. 6 (December 1990), https://doi.org/10.1086/261737.

29 Jim McKelvey, "Billionaire Jim McKelvey Reveals Secrets of Square's Record-Setting Pitch," Carmine Gallo, November 25, 2020, YouTube video, 25:49, https://www.youtube.com/watch?v=5enG-b39omw.

30 Ladan Shams and Aaron R. Seitz, "Benefits of Multisensory Learning," Trends in Cognitive Sciences 12, no. 11 (November 2008): 411–17, https://doi.org/10.1016/j.tics.2008.07.006.

31 Cheryl L. Grady et al., "Neural Correlates of the Episodic Encoding of Pictures and Words," PNAS 95, no. 5 (March 1998): 2703–8, https://doi.org/10.1073/pnas.95.5.2703; Snow et al., "Real-World Objects."

32 Valorie N. Salimpoor et al., "Anatomically Distinct Dopamine Release during Anticipation and Experience of Peak Emotion to Music," Nature Neuroscience 14 (January 2011): 257–62, https://doi.org/10.1038/nn.2726.

33 Julia Keller, "Pitch Is Paramount, Not Just in Showbiz," The Washington Post, September 4, 2003, https://www.washingtonpost.com/archive/lifestyle/2003/09/04/pitch-is-paramount-not-just-in-showbiz/e93e43f9-4beb-45f5-9f8f-4d19898f7414/.

34 Kimberly D. Elsbach, "How to Pitch a Brilliant Idea," Harvard Business Review, September 2003, https://hbr.org/2003/09/how-to-pitch-a-brilliant-idea.

35 "Meow Wolf: Origin Story SXSW 2018 Press Conference," Cara Mandel, March 12, 2018, YouTube video, 52:44, https://www.youtube.com/watch?v=voeeHvTg_Eo.

36 "Meow Wolf: Origin Story Trailer," Meow Wolf, accessed August 30, 2022, https://meowwolf.com/explore/origin-story.

37 McKelvey, "Billionaire Jim McKelvey Reveals Secrets."

38 Deborah A. Small, George Loewenstein, and Paul Slovic, "Sympathy and Callousness: The Impact of Deliberative Thought on Donations to Identifiable and Statistical Victims," Organizational Behavior and Human Decision Processes 102, no. 2 (March 2007): 143–53, https://doi.org/10.1016/j.obhdp.2006.01.005.